The Tramwɛ
Eastern Scotlanɑ
(Networks Edition)

This book, the twelfth in our regional series, and the first of two on Scotland, is based on Chapter 13 of *Great British Tramway Networks* by W. H. Bett and J. C. Gillham published in its fourth edition in 1962 and long out of print. For this enlarged version we are very grateful for the extensive help kindly provided by Alan Brotchie, Alastair Gunn, and Ian Souter.

We trace the history of tramways along both sides of the Firth of Forth, the north bank of the Firth of Tay, and as far north as Aberdeenshire. There were formerly thirteen tramway systems, plus several ancillary undertakings. These included three major cities, each of which had a progressive and profitable urban system and each had a link with an independent company which extended the City tramways on one or two routes further out into the countryside and encouraged the growth of suburbs. Our geographical sequence is from south to north, starting at Edinburgh and following the south bank of the Firth of Forth up to Stirling, where the river could easily be bridged. Returning along the north bank we travel eastwards through Dunfermline to Kirkcaldy and Wemyss, then head north to cross the Tay at Perth, and continue on to Dundee and Aberdeen. We end our tour well north of Aberdeen, at Cruden Bay, 110 miles as the crow flies north-east of our starting point.

Musselburgh

The visitor from the south following the east-coast route would come first to Musselburgh, a small town astride the River Esk, six miles east of Edinburgh. Here the Musselburgh & District Electric Light & Traction Co. Ltd., a subsidiary from 1905 of the National Electric Construction Co. Ltd., operated a tramway which had been built and opened by the NECC late in 1904, from the Edinburgh cable-tram terminus at Joppa, to Levenhall. This was extended along the coast to Port Seton in 1909, making a total of 6½ miles. Eventually there were 19 double-deck and three single-deck cars, including three of each type ex Sheffield Corporation. In 1923 through cars from Port Seton started to run over Corporation tracks to Edinburgh GPO, but early in 1928 the line from Port Seton to Levenhall was abandoned, and operation of Levenhall to Joppa was taken over by Edinburgh Corporation, who purchased it 3¼ years later, though the Company remained in business with motor buses and electricity supply until 1948. The tramcars were then sold off, and some bodies, including two ex-Sheffield single-deckers, were to be found close by the East Coast Main Line at Grantshouse fifty miles to the south until fairly recently.

Edinburgh

As one would expect, the largest system was at Edinburgh, and was owned latterly by the City Corporation. Under an Act of 1871 the Edinburgh Street Tramways Company was

Cover: Seen at the foot of The Mound, with Princes Street beyond, is Edinburgh 168 on an extra working of service 23 to Morningside Station. No. 168 was built at Shrubhill works in 1930 and survived until 1955. *(Roy Brook*

Back cover — Aberdeen

Above Sea Beach was a popular destination in the Summer. Ex-Manchester 50 is seen here awaiting departure in 1955. *(Roy Brook*

Below Aberdeen's newest trams were used on the trunk Bridges route. No. 27 is seen here at Bridge of Dee terminus on 3 August 1957. *(R. J. S. Wiseman*

The first sight of a tramcar for those travelling north on the old A1 up to 13 November 1954 would be at Levenhall. The ex-Manchester cars were used on this route, although No. 411, on an enthusiasts Special tour, is at Levenhall terminus in Ravenshaugh Road on 18 April 1954. *(R. J. S. Wiseman*

authorised to construct tramways in Edinburgh, Leith, and Portobello. It started operating in 1871 and had 32 horse-drawn cars three years later. By 1893 there were 84 cars and 18½ route miles, but at the end of that year Edinburgh Corporation purchased the 11¾ miles within the City boundary and immediately leased them to Dick Kerr & Co. Ltd. In 1898 the Portobello route, then outside the City, on which two steam trams had been used for a short time, was also sold to Edinburgh Corporation. Then in 1904 the five miles of route within the Burgh of Leith were sold to Leith Corporation, who also took over operation of them from the EST at the same time.

The Edinburgh Northern Tramways Company was formed by Dick Kerr & Co. Ltd. in 1884 to operate in some hilly parts of the town unsuitable for horse trams. Early in 1888 it opened the Hanover Street route with cable traction, Comely Bank following two years later. Both were bought in 1897 by Edinburgh Corporation, which leased them to Dick Kerr who had formed a new company, The Edinburgh & District Tramways Co. Ltd., to operate on lease all the lines of both the ENT Co. and also the former EST Co. systems. There was strong objection to overhead wires, especially on Princes Street, so the new Company at once started to convert all horse tramways to cable traction, as required by the terms of the lease, even though electric traction was now proven. In fact a demonstration line had been built in 1884 by Henry Binko for an international exhibition in Edinburgh. One of the horse cars of the District Company was equipped for electric operation, off a 'third rail', and ran the 700 yards from the Exhibition to the Haymarket Station.

The first route to be converted to cable, from Pilrig to St. Andrew Street, was opened in 1899, and thus split the through service between Edinburgh and Leith. By 1918 there were 211 eight-wheel double-deck cable cars, mostly open-top, working 25½ miles of route, including some new lines that had not been worked by horses, with 13 main and 12 auxiliary cables. The longest of the 13 was 33,600 feet long, or 6½ miles, which, when one visualises the innumerable vertical pulleys needed to support it in its conduit beneath the road surface, and the horizontal or angled pulleys needed to guide it round all the corners, also the complications at junctions and crossings, was a very wonderful piece of engineering.

The Leith and Edinburgh systems met at Pilrig at the junction of Leith Walk and Pilrig Street. No. 341 is heading down Leith Walk on service 25 to Kings Road, Portobello, via Leith. 20 April 1954. *(R. J. S. Wiseman*

The cables were endless, and ran at a fixed speed for the whole day, but gave trouble by breaking from time to time, and their other disadvantage was the rumbling noise made by all the pulleys. Each cable at some point along its route was diverted down a side street to reach the engine house and pass round the drum of a stationary engine which powered it, and there might have been a dozen or more heavily-loaded tramcars on any one cable at any one moment. Control was by a pair of jaws beneath the tram, known as a gripper, which passed through a slot in the road surface similar to the London conduit, and with these jaws the driver gripped or released the cable, which, unlike that of a cliff lift, was moving continuously, according to whether he wanted his car to move or stop.

The Edinburgh cable system was the fourth largest in the world, being exceeded only by San Francisco, Melbourne, and Kansas City. The Slateford route was a new extension, never served by horse or cable, and was opened in 1910 with four ex-cable cars which had been converted for overhead electric traction. The lease was for only 21 years and expired in 1919. As soon as it did, operation was taken over on 1 July 1919 by Edinburgh Corporation, who at once started to electrify all cable routes on the overhead principle. The first such conversion was Pilrig to Nether Liberton, which re-opened in 1922, and the entire job was finished in only 53 weeks. The little-used Morrison Street cable line was not electrified, and earlier there had been three very short horse sections which were not even cabled.

It will thus be seen that the Edinburgh electric tramway system was opened about 20 years later than most similar undertakings, so it was not surprising to find it by 1940 in a very efficient up-to-date and progressive state, with a high proportion of modern rolling stock. Two thirds of the fleet had been built or rebuilt since 1932, and further cars were built in the extensive Shrubhill workshops until 1950. The maximum fleet size was 360 cars, all covered-top four-wheelers, on 47¼ miles of 4′ 8½″ route. Between 1925 and 1937 the Edinburgh track mileage had increased by 14½% and the number of cars by 9½%, while the mileage of tramways in the country as a whole decreased by 38% and the number of cars by 24%. The main extensions were George Street, which made a relief line to Princes Street, Melville Drive, Craiglockhart to Colinton, and Seafield to Portobello (Kings Road). Further extensions were authorised in the Corporation's Provisional Order of 1934, but only the one from Braids to Fairmilehead was built, and although one to Crewe Toll was started in 1939 it was never completed.

Many of the newer Edinburgh cars had all-metal bodywork, which was very rare for trams though quite normal for buses even then, and some were of semi-streamlined shape. The entire fleet was painted in a livery of dark maroon for the main panels and a lighter brown for the window surrounds. All the fleet was still in good condition and the future seemed secure, and new trams were still being built until, quite suddenly, a change in outlook on the City Council, combined with the appointment of a new general manager, and the fact that some track was deteriorating produced a drastic change of policy in 1952, and the entire system, which had remained 100% intact until 1950, when one service was withdrawn but no track abandoned, was rapidly replaced by motor buses during the next 4½ years, 1952-56. Edinburgh with its many wide straight streets was especially suitable for tramways, and had been well served by them for about 80 years.

Pier Place, Newhaven, Leith, with two cars passing on the curves to Craighall Road before the opening of the Granton Circle. *(Commercial card courtesy A. W. Brotchie)*

Leith Corporation

The separation in 1904 of the Leith Tramways from those of Edinburgh has already been mentioned, but later they came back again. Leith Corporation owned and operated the horse lines from 1904, and electrified them on the overhead system in 1905, with an extension to Granton in 1909. There were eventually 37 double-deck four-wheel cars on nine miles of route. But the City of Edinburgh extended its boundaries in 1920 to include the Burgh of Leith, so the Leith tramways were automatically amalgamated with those of Edinburgh. The Leith electric trams met the Edinburgh cable cars at the boundary at Pilrig, where through passengers had to change. As soon as Edinburgh had electrified its cable tramway beyond the boundary at this point a new through service was inaugurated on 20 June 1922 and passengers no longer had to change cars.

Proposed Other Tramways

One of the City tram routes to the south terminated at Nether Liberton, and an Act of 1906 empowered a separate Edinburgh Suburban Electric Tramways Company to continue this for another seven miles to Eskbank, Dalkeith, and Bonnyrigg, but although the powers were renewed in 1911 they were eventually allowed to lapse. Another City tramway ended at Craiglockhart, from where the Colinton Tramways Company was authorised in 1909 to extend 1½ miles to Colinton village, with a ¾ mile branch to Slateford, most of the route to be on private right of way or roadside tramroad. Although this was never built Edinburgh Corporation did extend their Craiglockhart route 1½ miles to Colinton 17 years later, but as an ordinary street tramway.

There were also several proposals for a tramway to South Queensferry, none of which were authorised. The Edinburgh and Queensferry promoters applied in 1903 for a standard-gauge electric line from the western end of Princes Street, also from Goldenacre, along the whole length of the Queensferry Road, to end at the ferry landing stage close to the Forth Bridge, almost eight miles. This was refused, but a further application was made in 1905, backed by the National Electric group, in which the Princes Street connection was deleted and two other routes were proposed from the existing Newhaven Road and Comely Bank city tramways. These would unite at Davidsons Mains and continue to Queensferry as before, a total of almost 12 miles. The Edinburgh Suburban Electric Tramway Syndicate also proposed lines to the ferry, from Comely Bank terminus and from Bonnington Terrace via Ferry Road. As late as 1918 Edinburgh Corporation proposed a line from the West End and from Comely Bank, to continue to Port Edgar beyond the Ferry.

Winchburgh

At Winchburgh, three miles to the west of the Forth Bridge, there was from 1903 until 1961 a 2ft. 6in. gauge 500-volt electric tramway three miles long serving the shale-oil mines and plant of Scottish Oils Limited, formerly the Oakbank Oil Co. Ltd. There were six electric locomotives of four different types, with trolley-pole current collection, and five coaches for carrying employees to and from the several shale-oil mines and the refinery, as well as over 200 wagons for the shale itself.

Falkirk

Falkirk lies 24 miles west of Edinburgh and 22 east of Glasgow. It developed as a market town, and in the mid-18th century the iron industry arrived, helped by the building of the Forth & Clyde canal and later the railways. Proposals for tramways were mooted early in 1900, and were authorised by the Falkirk & District Tramways Order Confirmation Act of 1901. The statutory Falkirk & District Tramways Company thus created failed to construct the tramway, and the Company passed in 1904 to ownership by the Falkirk Electric Construction Syndicate Limited, a subsidiary of Bruce Peebles & Co. Ltd. of Edinburgh. Both Falkirk companies co-existed for many years, but from 1920 onwards under the ownership of the Fife Tramway Light & Power Co. Ltd., which already owned the Dunfermline tramways.

The tramway was opened on 21 October 1905, and was a 6¼ mile circular route connecting Falkirk and Larbert with Camelon and the famous Carron Ironworks. It was laid to the four-foot gauge, and had ten major bridges including two heavy swing bridges over the canal with tramway catch points on each side. From Falkirk itself, on the south-eastern corner of the circle, a 1½ mile branch, opened later and closed earlier than the rest, extended to Laurieston, but a longer and potentially more profitable four-mile authorised route to beyond Grangemouth, where new industry was developing on the banks of the Forth, was not constructed.

THE CROSS, LARBERT.

The Cross, Larbert. The tram, of series 1-15, is turning left out of Main Street en-route to Falkirk. The track in the foreground was possibly intended for a line towards Stirling.
(Commercial card

There were many lengths of single track and loops on the original layout, so on the three days of the Tryst Fair in 1907 an intensive service was run anti-clockwise round the circle thus avoiding delays at the loops and reducing the journey time for the circuit from 45 to 38 minutes. The tracks were rebuilt with more double lines in the 1920's, and with the arrival of ten modern single-deck bogie cars in 1929 replacing the original 18 open-top cars (15 French and 3 by Brush) which were worn out and not strong enough to take top covers, the tramway carried increasing numbers of passengers. As a result of this success four more new single-deckers and five secondhand ones from the Dearne District Light Railways were purchased in 1931-34, and a four-minute service was offered at weekends.

The Fife TL&P Company, with its Falkirk and Dunfermline subsidiaries, was bought out in 1935 by the Scottish Motor Traction Co. Ltd. and sadly the Falkirk trams were replaced by W. Alexander & Sons Ltd. motor buses in 1936. The new trams never ran again, but many were sold off as holiday homes, and No. 14 was later rescued and is now partly restored and in store at Grangemouth.

Stirling

Situated at the head of the Forth Estuary, Stirling commands the routes from the Highlands to the Scottish Lowlands and thus developed as a road and railway centre. The Stirling & Bridge of Allan Tramways Co. Ltd. opened a standard-gauge horse tramway 3½ miles long from the health resort at Bridge of Allan to the railway station at Stirling on 30 July 1874, which was extended one mile southwards to St. Ninians on 29 January 1898. A variety of single-deck and double-deck tramcars, some secondhand from Glasgow or Edinburgh, served the line over the years, one of which, open-top car No. 22, was fitted with a Commer petrol engine in 1913. Latterly there were 14 cars and 45 horses.

Several proposals to electrify were made, but all fell through for one reason or another. First was the British Electric Traction Co. Ltd., with a scheme in 1899 to electrify the line and extend it, partly as a light railway, to Dollar, ten miles, but negotiations fell through in 1902. Another proposal was made in 1906 by the National Electric Construction Co. Ltd., for a 3ft. 6in. gauge line from Dunblane via the existing route south to Bannockburn, eight miles in total. The Town Council also considered buying the tramway, until finally Balfour Beatty & Co. Ltd. were invited, in 1913, to submit proposals. After their success in Dunfermline and elsewhere Balfour Beatty suggested lengthy lines out to Larbert, Denny, Alloa, and Dollar, but nothing came of these even though in 1905 a junction had been put in at Larbert on the Falkirk tramway system, pointing in the Stirling direction.

The tramway survived for a further seven years, the horse cars running for the last time on 5 February 1920, and the petrol tram three months later on 20 May. The Company sold out to the Scottish General Omnibus Co. Ltd., which had been created in 1919 as the bus-operating subsidiary of the Falkirk & District Tramways Company, and commenced operations in 1919 on the run from Bridge of Allan to Bannockburn, eventually selling out in 1930 to W. Alexander & Sons Ltd.

Dunfermline

The Royal Burgh of Dunfermline, county town of Fife and one-time capital of Scotland, 20 miles east of Stirling, is situated on higher ground to the north of the Firth of Forth. Renowned for the quality of its linen manufacture the town prospered, and during the 19th century the development of the Fife coalfield resulted in a rapidly growing population in the adjacent villages to the east. It was not until 1903, however, that plans for tramways were first put forward, by the National Electric Construction Co. Ltd. These did not materialise, but eventually the Dunfermline & District Tramways Company, incorporated in 1906, and after 1909 a subsidiary of the Fife Tramway Light & Power Co. Ltd., obtained powers to construct tramways in the district. In the early days George Balfour was a director of the Fife, Falkirk, Dunfermline, Wemyss, Broughty Ferry, and Dumbarton tramway companies as a private individual, but none of these companies were themselves owned or controlled by Balfour Beatty & Co. Ltd. as a company.

Dunfermline's first, and main line, to Cowdenbeath, opened on 2 November 1909, followed the next day by the steeply-graded local line to Townhill. Cowdenbeath was extended to Lochgelly in December, and with the granting of further powers new lines were opened to Kelty, partly on reserved track, in 1910, and to Lochore in December 1912. The Rumblingwell line, to the north-west of the town, was opened in December 1913, but a Lochgelly to Kinglassie route authorised by Act of 1915 was not built.

Tramways to Rosyth by three different routes had been proposed, in 1906, 1910, and 1915, and those of 1910 and 1915 were authorised. The latter alternative, via Queensferry Road, 3¼ miles long and mostly reserved track, was opened on 17 May 1918. This was urgently needed by now to serve the new Naval Dockyard then being built at Rosyth, and the Government contributed one-fifth of the estimated cost of its construction. Fifteen more cars and a new depot at St. Leonards were also needed for the extension. This brought the total route length up to 18¼ miles, and the maximum fleet size a few years later was 45 cars, all four-wheel double-deckers.

The main line was a long inter-urban route serving four colliery villages and three towns with 34 passing loops plus three short lengths of double track, and involved a journey of 65 minutes at an average speed of a little over nine miles per hour for the ten-mile journey. The fleet of 28 older and 15 newer trams could not compete with motor buses under these conditions, and so during 1921-30 the line was doubled, with some

Dunfermline No. 36 on the reserved track of the Rosyth route opened in 1918.
(National Tramway Museum

roadside reserved track, and the journey time drastically improved, so much so that by 1937 Dunfermline had the fastest scheduled average speed in Britain, but sadly the fleet was not updated to match. In 1925 work was about to start on an extension to Inverkeithing when it was announced that the Dockyard was to close. As late as 1926 an Act was passed authorising a 2½ mile extension from Lochgelly to Cardenden on private right-of-way, but this was not built. Although Cowdenbeath to Kelty was abandoned in 1931 the Company had no intention of abandoning its profitable tramways, and the Lochore track was extended 100 yards in 1930. But the Scottish Motor Traction Co. Ltd. purchased the share capital of the Fife company in 1935, and Alexander's buses replaced the Dunfermline trams in 1937.

Kirkcaldy

Kirkcaldy developed on the north bank of the Firth of Forth, and was famous for exporting coal, also for making linoleum, which it still does today. Tramways were proposed as early as 1883, when the Kirkcaldy & District Tramways Act authorised routes to West Bridge, Dysart, and the railway station, just over 3¼ miles in total, to be worked by steam on the 3ft. 6in. gauge. But the capital could not be raised and the scheme lapsed. The Town Council was keen to own a tramway, and in 1898 it applied for an Act of Parliament. This was granted in 1899, but construction was delayed, and it was not until February 1903 that the West Bridge to Gallatown service opened, on 3ft. 6in. gauge. This was followed by the "Upper Route" serving the railway station, and a short branch to Beveridge Park Gates. Another short branch, to Dysart, under a mile long, was opened in January 1911, bringing the total to just over six miles, but although three other lines had been authorised by Act of 1903 no further extensions were built.

In 1909 the National Electric Construction Co. Ltd. proposed a tramway from Rosyth to Kirkcaldy's Park Gates terminus, via Inverkeithing, Aberdour, and Burntisland, but it missed the Parliamentary deadline and was not revived for the next or any subsequent Session. The Dunfermline company obtained powers in 1915 to extend from Lochgelly to Kinglassie, where it would have joined the authorised Wemyss tramway extension from Kirkcaldy (Gallatown) via Thornton. Had these proposals been carried out an unbroken chain of tramways would have extended for 30 miles from Rosyth and Dunfermline to Methil and Leven, although only 21 as the crow flies.

In contrast to the Rosyth route Kirkcaldy trams had to run through some very narrow streets. No. 17 is near Links terminus. *(E. O. Catford, courtesy A. W. Brotchie*

A total of 26 four-wheel open-top trams, mostly supplied by G. F. Milnes & Co. Ltd., operated Kirkcaldy's small but efficiently run municipal tramway. Its future was considered in 1929, and the Manager reported on the merits, and costs, of tramway modernisation, trolleybuses, and municipal motor buses. In the event, however, the trams were replaced on 15 May 1931 by a separate self-contained fleet of motor buses operated by W. Alexander & Sons Ltd. on behalf of the Corporation for an annual payment of £2,000 for 21 years, later renewed for another 21 years, on a leasehold arrangement seen elsewhere only at Perth, Gloucester and Worcester. This however was not quite the end at Kirkcaldy, for Wemyss trams continued to work as far as Gallatown for eight more months.

Wemyss

Extensive coal reserves lay beneath the rich agricultural countryside north of the Forth estuary, also below it, and northeast of Kirkcaldy. These were exploited by the Wemyss Estate from the mid-17th century onwards. Pits were sunk, and new model villages to house the miners were built between Kirkcaldy and Leven. Railway services from Methil or Leven to Kirkcaldy and Edinburgh via Thornton Junction were indirect, and so plans for a direct tramway line to Kirkcaldy were discussed from late 1904 onwards. The North British Railway rejected an invitation to build and run this, and later opposed its construction. So with the enthusiastic financial support of Randolph, the Laird of Wemyss, the Wemyss & District Tramways Co. Ltd. was registered in Edinburgh in 1905, and an Act was obtained later that year for a tramway from Leven via Methil and Wemyss to join the Kirkcaldy tram terminus at Gallatown. A branch from Coaltown to Dysart, where it would have joined another Kirkcaldy terminus, was authorised but not built.

The line as built, not quite 7½ miles from Leven to Gallatown, on 3ft. 6in. gauge, was a true inter-urban, with street track along the narrow village streets, private right-of-way across the Wemyss Estate, and single line with loops at roughly half-mile intervals. Adding to its splendour were the views across the Firth of Forth to Edinburgh and the hills beyond. The line was entirely financed by Randolph Wemyss, and opened on 1 September 1906 with nine four-wheel single-deck cars with vestibuled ends and clerestory roofs, rather American in appearance, augmented the following year by four similar cars. Permission to run trailers was given, but there is no evidence that they were ever built or used, except for parcels. An Act of 1910 gave the Wemyss company powers to build 11½ miles of tramway from Gallatown via Thornton and Kinglassie to Lochgelly, where it would have joined the Dunfermline tramways . None of this was built, even though an Act of 1915 transferred the powers for Kinglassie to Lochgelly to the Dunfermline company.

The Wemyss company prospered, and to speed up the service much of the track was doubled in 1914, to give six sections of ballasted sleeper track, four roadside and two fenced in and running on private land, although Wellesley Road, Methil, was converted to a public street. With four new larger bogie cars obtained in 1907 and two in 1925 the time for the through journey was reduced from 75 to 60 minutes. The depot was at Aberhill, but two cars were kept nightly by Kirkcaldy Corporation in their depot for early morning eastbound journeys. Wemyss had running powers over 2½ miles of Kirkcaldy track from Gallatown into the town centre, and worked a through service. Bus competition became severe from mid-1922 onwards, but the trams were still profitable up to 1928 even though the Company was now running its own buses, and two more bogie trams were bought, bringing the total to 21. But the company was purchased by Alexanders and sadly the trams ran for the last time on 30 January 1932, being replaced the next day by Alexander's buses.

Double track was laid in Leven High Street. The local children appear to be welcoming Wemyss tramcar No. 1; probably on the opening day, 25 August 1906.
(A. W. Brotchie Collection

Perth City

Perth, another former capital of Scotland, developed as a port around the lowest bridge crossing the River Tay, and prospered as a market town for the surrounding agricultural area, with dyeing and whisky-blending industries. A horse-bus service to Scone, 2¼ miles away across the bridge, was started in the 1860's and was succeeded in 1895 by a horse tramway owned by the Perth & District Tramways Co. Ltd., who extended the line beyond the railway station ¼-mile along the Glasgow Road, and in 1898 another half mile to Cherrybank, and also built a short branch to Craigie.

This tramway was taken over by Perth Corporation on 7 October 1903 and rebuilt for electric traction, the new trams replacing the horse cars during the afternoon of 31 October 1905. A half-mile branch to Dunkeld Road was built, but half-mile extensions authorised in 1908 to Dovecot Land and along Crieff Road, also to Magdalen Bank, only 335 yards beyond Craigie terminus, were not built. Twelve open-top single-truck cars were supplied by Hurst Nelson & Co. Ltd. and housed in the depot at the Scone terminus. This small compact system of one long and three short routes, totalling just five miles, on 3ft. 6in. gauge, then settled down to 20 uneventful years until it was replaced by Corporation motor buses on 19 January 1929. These were taken over in May 1934 by W. Alexander & Sons, Ltd. on a 21 year lease, with a separate self-contained fleet painted in a dark red livery instead of Alexander's normal medium blue. The tram depot, complete with tracks, remained intact until quite recently.

Almondbank

Four miles to the north-west of Perth a short standard-gauge electrified industrial line was built in October 1911 from Almondbank Station, on the Crieff branch of the Caledonian Railway, to serve two large bleach works of Lumsden & Mackenzie Limited at Huntingtowerfield and Pitcairnfield, about a mile to the north. The single line, with two passing loops, was worked by an English Electric "box-cab" locomotive using overhead current collection by pantograph at 500 volts dc, which had two 25 hp Dick Kerr motors and a Westinghouse tramcar-type controller, but it closed on 8 November 1962.

Dalmunzie

About 27 miles due north of Perth, near the Spital of Glenshee, a privately-owned railway of 2ft. 6in. gauge and about 2½ miles long was built to connect Dalmunzie House, now a hotel, with the nearby grouse moor. The single-track line climbed 500 feet with severe gradients and a double-reverse zig-zag on the steepest part, and was worked by petrol-paraffin 20 hp Simplex engines, driven by a gamekeeper when required. The two coaches seated four on upholstered seats, and eight, respectively.

Inchture

The Perth to Dundee Railway, part of the Caledonian system from 1865, was built on the flat land to the north of the Firth of Tay, and by-passed the villages of Errol and Inchture. It had been suggested that branch lines should be built to serve each village, but the line to Errol south of the main line was never seriously intended, although that to Inchture (Crossgates), 1½ miles north of Inchture Railway Station, was opened in 1850. This was worked by a one-horse tramcar built at St. Rollox in 1895 to replace the old four-wheeled coach used originally. The single track was extended a further half-mile or so in about 1870 to serve a brick works and a clay pit, but this was disused from 1900 and dismantled, and the rest of the line closed in 1916. The line to Errol was never built.

Dundee City Tramways

The City of Dundee, initially a market town on the north bank of the Firth of Tay, and bordered by steeply rising hills to the north, expanded during the 19th century to become a major port, and a centre of the jute spinning industry based on the import of raw material from Calcutta. Horse tramways were introduced on 30 August 1877 by the Dundee & District Tramways Co. Ltd., from the City Centre along the Perth Road as far as Windsor Street, using cars hired from Edinburgh and Glasgow. Two years later this was extended to West Park, and new lines were built to Lochee, Stobswell, and Baxter Park. Steam traction was introduced in 1884 on a new line to Fairmuir via Dens Road and Hilltown, which was steeply inclined and for which cable trams had been proposed in 1881. Steam also appeared in 1885 on the Lochee route, a stiff climb for horses, and later on the lines to Stobswell and Baxter Park, with a total of 13 locomotives by Thos. Green & Sons Ltd.

Dundee Corporation, which had always owned the tracks, took over operation on 1 June 1899, and proceeded to electrify and extend the system. No time was lost, and electric trams were running to West Park by 13 July 1900 and to Lochee on 22 October 1900. All other routes were electric by the end of May 1902, except for short sections in Victoria Street and Dura Street, and along Morgan Street to Stobswell. These three were replaced by new electrified lines through to Maryfield via King Street and Albert Street, and to Baxter Park via King Street. The Lochee line was extended a short way, West Park was extended to Ninewells, and Fairmuir one mile to Downfield. New lines were built, notably the steeply-graded line to Hilltown via Constitution Road and Barrack Road, worked by six single-deck four-motor bogie cars, although cable traction had been proposed in 1902. A new route was built to Blackness, paralleling the Ninewells line but 200 feet above it, and the total route mileage now reached 16½, all on standard gauge. The last new extension was a short single line in Lindsay Street opened on 3 July 1933 to allow Lochee cars to terminate around a city-centre loop. The main car works was in Lochee Road near the city centre, with running depots here and at Maryfield and Lochee High Street.

From 1912 to 1914 two Railless trolleybuses worked 1¼ miles along Clepington Road from Maryfield to Fairmuir, and, apart from Glasgow, these were the only trolleybuses ever used in Scotland, where they did not find so much favour as in England. An Act of 1925 authorised a tramway extension from Maryfield for a short distance along the new Kingsway, and a connection from Fairmuir to Lochee via Johnston Avenue and Loons Road, but these were not built. Dundee is a city of hills, and the trams had to negotiate steep gradients and tight curves, except for the routes parallel to the Tay, i.e. Ninewells, Blackness, and Baxter Park. Thus the routes northwards to Lochee and Downfield climbed for most of the way with maximum gradients of 1-in-11 and 1-in-10 respectively.

All the routes were still operating in 1953, except the Constitution Road line and the short routes to Craig Pier and Baxter Park, which had been abandoned in 1928, 1919, and 1932 respectively, as also had the Broughty Ferry route described later. The tramways were maintained in excellent condition until the end of 1955, when, suddenly, following the appointment of a new manager, the Blackness and Downfield routes were abandoned in November 1955, said at the time to be temporarily. Less than a year later all the other routes were replaced by secondhand motor-buses from London Transport. By 27 October 1956, when the last tram ran from Maryfield to Lochee, Dundee had become the last traditional tramway in Great Britain, with Ninewells being the last street tramway to be mainly single track and loops. The rolling stock was traditional, latterly all totally-enclosed four-wheel double-deckers, with a maximum of 96 in 1925. The oldest cars, much rebuilt, dated from 1900, and the newest, the Lochee cars built by Brush in 1930, were very fast and comfortable.

Dundee was the last tramway system with single line and loops to be closed. On 2 August 1955 No. 46 is passing Lochee car No. 24 on the West Park loop.
(R. J. S. Wiseman

Dundee Electricity Works

A new generating station was built in 1908 for Dundee Corporation at Stannergate, and was linked to the railway exchange sidings by about 1,500 yards of track electrified on the overhead system at 420 volts d.c. (2 by 210v). The four-wheeled locomotive with twin trolleys was built by the United Electric Car Co. Ltd. at Preston, and had two GE52 6T motors of 25 hp and K2 controllers. This was replaced by a battery-driven locomotive in 1930, but remained on stand-by duty until 1963 when the overhead was dismantled.

Broughty Ferry

The fishing village of Broughty Ferry on the northern bank of the Firth of Tay 3½ miles east of Dundee developed in the late 19th century as a residential area for Dundee's more affluent citizens anxious to move out from the congested city centre. It was also popular as a summer seaside resort, and a tramway was proposed as early as 1872 under the Dundee Tramways Act of that year. An electric light railway was promoted by Greenwood & Batley Limited in 1898, but the Board of Trade would not confirm the Order under the Light Railways Act due to the opposition of the Dundee & Arbroath Joint Railway (Caledonian and North British). Undaunted, in 1900 the Company promoted a Bill for a line as far as Carnoustie, eleven miles, but this was withdrawn. An earlier proposal for a line as far as Arbroath, 16 miles from Dundee or 19 from Ninewells, also failed to engender enough interest. But the potential for a tramway was still there, and with the help of Mr. George Balfour of Balfour Beatty & Co. Ltd. an Act was passed in 1904, and the Dundee, Broughty Ferry & District Tramways Co. Ltd. was registered in 1905.

The line was a continuation of a Dundee Corporation line beyond Craigie Terrace, and extended 5¼ miles from here through Broughty Ferry to Monifieth, mainly double track, and included ¾ mile of sleeper track through the private Craigie Estate, with running powers over 1½ miles of Corporation tramway. This opened on 27 December 1905, and was worked jointly with Dundee Corporation from a city terminus in Seagate. It was extended a short distance along Monifieth High Street in 1908, but was shortened by one

16

On 15 May 1931 the last trams ran to Broughty Ferry and Monifieth. No. 14 awaits departure from Seagate terminus, Dundee. A Corporation Leyland Titan TD1 bus is in the background. *(D. C. Thomson*

mile to 4¼ in 1914 when the section between Craigie Terrace and Belsize Road was purchased by Dundee Corporation when the City boundaries were extended, thus increasing the running powers to 2½ miles. The line offered fine views of the Tay estuary, and the success of the company depended very much on the weather, for on fine summer Sundays traffic to the local beaches was very heavy. This route also served five golf courses, and at one stage it offered golfers a special 6d return ticket to Monifieth.

The line was opened initially with twelve open-topped uncanopied four-wheel cars, of which two were later top-covered, and these together with two further cars purchased in 1906 maintained the winter service. Two more cars were bought secondhand from Dundee Corporation in 1926. Later, trolleybuses or a modernised tramway were considered, but, instead, the Company was purchased by Dundee Corporation on 16 May 1931, and twelve Corporation motor buses took over on the same day.

Aberdeen City

Some 71 miles north-east of Dundee by railway, 66 by road, but only 58 direct, is the city of Aberdeen, the third city of Scotland, a major urban centre which developed around the mouth of the River Dee. By the middle of the 19th century it had expanded beyond its congested centre, and proposals for tramways were first made in 1871. The Aberdeen District Tramways Act was passed in August 1872, and the first routes, to Kittybrewster and to Queens Cross, both from King Street, opened on 31 August 1874. Following much local controversy over a bid by the Great North of Scotland Railway Company to purchase the system, the Company sold out to Aberdeen Corporation, who took over on 26 August 1898. By this time standard-gauge horse trams were running to Bridge of Don, Bridge of Dee, Woodside, Mannofield, Rubislaw (beyond Queens Cross), and round the Rosemount Circle.

Electrification was quickly put in hand, and on 23 December 1899 electric trams were inaugurated on the Woodside route, the conversion process being completed within 2½ years. Each route had its own depot, and, initially, its own set of open-top cars as in horse-tram practice, each numbered in a separate series from 1 up. By 1903 new routes had been opened to Sea Beach, Torry, Ferryhill and Duthie Park. The system prospered over the years, the fleet was continually upgraded, halfpenny fares were a success, and the Pay-as-you-Enter fare system was introduced on the Woodside route in 1913 and extended to some others, but scrapped in 1915.

The system reached its maximum of 15¼ route miles in 1924 when the Rubislaw route was extended from Bayview Road to Woodend, and thence, on reserved track, to Hazlehead Park. The weakest and shortest routes, to Torry, Ferryhill, and Duthie Park, all in the south-east, were abandoned in 1931. The Suburban Company (see later) continued the tramway beyond Woodside, but abandoned its line in 1927, although in 1938 a short part, as far as the City Boundary at Scatterburn, was re-opened by the Corporation. Much work was done in 1939 on rebuilding the Sea Beach route, which carried a heavy summer traffic, onto a more direct reserved-track alignment, but delays in building a new railway bridge alongside the old one, also the demolition of some buildings, and then the war, meant that this work was never completed.

The Aberdeen tram fleet reached its maximum of 118 in 1929. All were traditional single-truck double-deck cars built locally or by Brush or BEC, earlier ones being open-balconied and later ones enclosed. The fleet was strengthened in 1936 by the purchase of eighteen all-enclosed cars from Nottingham only ten years old. Four splendid new streamlined double-deck trams were purchased in 1940; two were four-wheelers with end entrances and two were high-capacity eight-wheelers with central entrances. An order was placed for twenty more bogie cars, but these were not delivered until after the war in 1949. Meantime as a stop-gap measure fifteen Pilcher Pullman cars were purchased from Manchester in 1948.

Aberdeen was a fine example of a progressive transport undertaking which made maximum use of its investment in its tramways at least until 1955. The hub of the system was Castle Street, and all services except those to Scatterburn, ran via Union Street, an important shopping street on which tracks were relaid in 1946. The terminus for the Woodside and Scatterburn services was in the narrow St. Nicholas Street, where trams could easily reverse. The last route to be abandoned, the Bridge of Don to Bridge of Dee

Twenty streamlined bogie cars were built for Aberdeen in 1949. No. 20 on the Bridges route in Union Street, 4 August 1955. *(J. C. Gillham)*

trunk line, was double track throughout, on wide straight uncongested roads, and worked latterly by magnificent modern bogie cars. All the main routes were kept in good condition until 1951, when Mannofield was replaced by Corporation motor buses, and the others followed at roughly yearly intervals from 1954, when the abandonment decision was taken, until final closure in May 1958 brought the system to an end, condemning the surviving fleet, including the luxurious bogie cars, barely ten years old, to a mass conflagration on the Beach tracks after closure. The depot at Queens Cross, rebuilt and enlarged in 1951, was converted into studios for Grampian television, surely a most unusual fate.

Aberdeen Suburban

To serve the developing residential and industrial communities beyond the Aberdeen city boundary fairly close to the Rivers Don and Dee, two electric tramways, isolated from each other, were proposed in 1901, as extensions from the Corporation's termini at Woodside to Bankhead and at Mannofield to Peterculter. Thus the Aberdeen Suburban Tramways Order Confirmation Act was passed on 31 July 1902, but due to lack of finance construction was delayed. The north-western (Donside) line to Bankhead, two miles, was opened on 23 June 1904, and the south-western (Deeside) line, as far as Bieldside, 2¼ miles, followed on 7 July, but the 3¼ miles from Bieldside to the intended terminus at Peterculter was never completed. Both lines extended inside the City boundary, the northern one by half a mile and the southern one by 100 yards at first, but later (soon after abandonment) by 1¼ miles when the boundary was moved. Both services operated with running powers through to St. Nicholas Street or Castle Street as an integral part of the Corporation's own services.

The initial fleet of six was a mixture of open-top and uncanopied top-covered cars, all with fully-vestibuled platforms from the onset, and separate smoking and non-smoking saloons in the lower deck. Three later cars from UEC of Preston were of conventional British balcony-car design but again with fully-vestibuled platforms. To cater for the summer excursion traffic single-deck toastrack trailers were proposed for week-end use on the Deeside line, but although approved by the Board of Trade the Company bought balcony cars 10 and 11 in 1911/1914 instead.

The Suburban company was reasonably successful in its early years, and on two occasions, in 1914 and 1923, Aberdeen Corporation offered to buy its lines and integrate the services with its own, but terms could not be agreed. By 1925 the Company's tracks and trams were in poor condition, and with capital unavailable for investment in track renewal and rolling stock it was unable to remedy the situation. The vehicles deteriorated to such an extent that the Corporation ended the through-running agreement in June 1926, and the Company then maintained a local service on each line. An increasingly spasmodic operation continued for another year on both lines, with the last cars running on the Donside line on 2 July 1927, while on Deeside No. 11 shuttled back and forth for about one more week. Replacement was by buses of the associated Aberdeen Suburban Transport Co. Ltd., which was itself bought in 1932 by W. Alexander & Sons Ltd. Bankhead, half a mile north of the Bridge of Don, was the most northerly point reached by street tramcars in the British Isles.

In 1938, eleven years after abandonment, Aberdeen Corporation re-instated the first half mile of the Bankhead route by extending its own tramway from Woodside as far as the City boundary at Scatterburn. This did not happen at Mannofield, where the tramway ownership boundary was only slightly short of the City boundary, and in 1929 Corporation tram tracks were extended about 100 yards to close this gap.

The most northerly point anywhere reached by a double-deck tramcar was the terminus of the Aberdeen Suburban Company's line to Bankhead. No. 4 is in original condition. *(I. A. Souter*

Strabathie and Murcar

Immediately north of the Bridge of Don was the terminus of a three-foot gauge line built by the Seaton Brick & Tile Co. Ltd., to connect Aberdeen with their brickworks at Blackdog three miles to the north. It was opened in 1899, and to transport the workforce as well as offering a public passenger service horse cars, displaced by electrification, were purchased from Aberdeen Corporation in 1900. These were hauled by a Hudswell Clarke 0-4-0 ST steam engine, but from 1909 passenger services were provided by a four-wheeled petrol-engined railcar built by J. B. Duff in Aberdeen. When the brickworks closed in 1924 the tramway beyond Murcar was abandoned and the remainder was acquired and operated by Murcar Golf Club. The original petrol car had been extensively rebuilt in 1918, and was joined in 1932 by a new 40-seat four-wheeled petrol railcar built by D. Wickham & Co. of Ware, Hertfordshire. The line survived until 1951.

Other Minor Aberdeen Lines

At Aberdeen the Harbour Railways included a street-running extension to the Corporation Gas Works of 1887, via a half-mile route from the Waterloo GNSR goods station, along Church Street, St. Clement Street, and Miller Street. This was worked until the 1960's by steam engines with the motion enclosed, and lasted until the 1980's. There was also a lengthy line via Market Street and North Esplanade connecting the Docks with the Corporation electricity generating station opened in 1925 at Dee Village (Ferryhill). This supplied both Company and Corporation tramways with power, and on which Dick Kerr or English Electric battery locomotives were used until 1969. At Peterculter an industrial line with 500-volt tramway-type equipment and twin overhead wires was located at the Culter Paper Mills, and worked from 1897 to 1920 with a Dick Kerr four-wheel locomotive.

Further north was the Cruden Bay Hotel Tramway. The laundry, which served all GNSR Hotels, was still extant, as were the ornate tram standards, in 1955.   *(J. C. Gillham*

The Grampian Transport Museum at Alford, 24 miles west of Aberdeen, houses the Aberdeen horse tram and a Cruden Bay Hotel car which is currently (1999) being restored. The adjacent two-foot gauge Alford Valley Railway deploys the lower saloon of Aberdeen Suburban No. 11 as a trailer car. At Stonehaven, 14 miles south of Aberdeen, it has been suggested that there was once a street horse tramway in the early 1900's, but this is wrong; it was only a horse bus service.

Cruden Bay

Twenty miles north of Aberdeen the Great North of Scotland Railway opened a hotel and golf course at Cruden Bay in the spring of 1899, on the recently-opened Ellon to Boddam branch of the railway. The hotel was over half a mile from the station, so after inspecting the tramways in the Isle of Man the railway company decided to build a tramway to convey guests and luggage to the hotel. As the hotel was also to serve as the central laundry for all the Company's hotels and restaurants, laundry baskets were a significant part of the traffic. This 3ft. 6½in. gauge line, which opened on 1 June 1899, was single, and ballasted sleeper reserved track with bullhead rails, except for tarmac instead of ballast where it crossed the main Port Erroll road. It ended in front of the hotel, with a branch to the car shed and laundry and other out-buildings at the rear. The two clerestoried combination-type electric tramcars, with accommodation for passengers and luggage, and two trailers, were built at the Kittybrewster Works of the GNSR, and in 1922 passed to the LNER. The passenger service, mainly for golfers and hotel guests, ceased on 1 November 1932 when the Boddam branch railway lost its passenger trains. The tramway continued to carry goods and laundry baskets until 31 December 1940, when the hotel was requisitioned by the Army, and it was dismantled soon afterwards, as was the railway at the end of 1948.

Aberdeen County Proposals

The County of Aberdeen is a very large one, stretching 40 miles north of the City, and it contained quite a lot of proposals for rural light railways, but only one of these was ever built. Several rural steam tramways, mostly centered on the City, were proposed in 1876 but none were ever authorised. Many others were proposed under the Light Railways Act of 1896 but only one of these was authorised, and they mostly floundered on their inability to negotiate passage through urban areas. One was for a tramway from Echt, a village 13 miles west of Aberdeen, to join the City tramways at Rubislaw (Bayview) and run over them into the city centre. There was an Aberdeen - Garlogie - Echt GNSR proposal, 13 miles, in 1896, Aberdeen - Skene - Echt also in 1896, and Aberdeen - Dunecht - Echt, 15 miles, in 1899. These Echt proposals included standard and narrow gauge with steam and electric options. Other proposed tramways or light railways, probably all steam, included Aberdeen to Newburgh, 12 miles along the coast, GNSR 1896; Logierieve - Tarves - Methlick (electric), 9 miles, GNSR 1900; Maud - New Pitsligo - Turriff, 15 miles, 1913; Fraserburgh - New Aberdour, 8 miles, 1897; Fraserburgh - Rosehearty - New Aberdour, about 9 miles, and Fraserburgh - Rosehearty, 4½ miles, GNSR, 1908. Details of some of these, all well to the north of the City, are rather vague.

The West Buchan Light Railway was to run east from Turriff via the public road towards Cuminestown, Garmond, and New Byth, then across country to New Pitsligo, along the length of the main street here, then roadside to Brucklay GNSR station. The gauge was originally to be 2ft. 6in., later 3ft. 0in., and the total length 21½ miles. Electric traction was seriously considered, and the route varied slightly with time, and it was still under consideration until the early 1920's. Of all the foregoing the only line to be approved and authorised (under the 1896 Act) was the Fraserburgh and St. Combs Light Railway Order of 1899, for a 4½ mile line closely hugging the coastline around the north-eastern corner of the County. This was opened by the GNSR in 1903 as a conventional steam railway although powers were held for electric traction. It closed in 1965 with diesel traction.

Hopeman and Inverness

At Cummingstown, on the Moray coast six miles north-west of Elgin, at the end of a Highland Railway branch line, Sir William Gordon Cumming was authorised by an Act of 1901 to build the 1¼ mile Hopeman Tramway, to Clashach to serve his quarries, with an electric power station, but this project fell through. We are now only about 35 miles from Inverness, but despite the size and importance of this town it never had any tramways, nor any authorised unbuilt lines. Early in 1903 the citizens at a public meeting resolved to form a company to build and operate horse tramways from the railway station to Kessock Ferry, Ness Island, and Millburn, to be electrified later if a public electricity supply should become available, but nothing further was heard of this.

Aberdeen intended to rebuild the Sea Beach route on a new Boulevard. Work started in 1939 and tracks were laid in Bannermill Road, but never used. They were lifted in 1958.
(J. C. Gillham

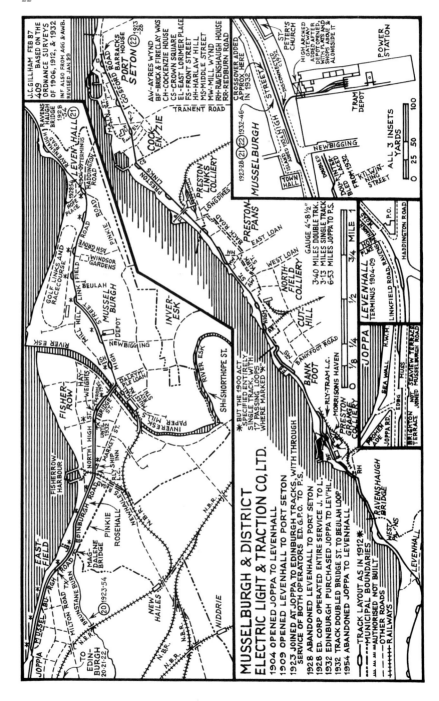

MUSSELBURGH & DISTRICT ELECTRIC LIGHT & TRACTION CO. LTD.

1904 OPENED JOPPA TO LEVENHALL
1909 OPENED LEVENHALL TO PORT SETON
1923 JOINED AT JOPPA TO EDINBURGH TRACKS, WITH THROUGH SERVICE OF BOTH OPERATORS ED. G.P.O. TO P.S.
1928 ABANDONED LEVENHALL TO PORT SETON
1928 ED. CORP OPERATED ENTIRE SERVICE J. TO L.
1932 EDINBURGH PURCHASED JOPPA TO LEV'HLL.
1932 TRACK DOUBLED BRIDGE ST. TO BEULAH LOOP
1954 ABANDONED JOPPA TO LEVENHALL

—————— TRACK LAYOUT AS IN 1912 ✳
·—··—··—· MUNICIPAL BOUNDARIES
⊔⊔⊔⊔⊔⊔ AUTHORISED NOT BUILT
- - - - OTHER ROADS
+++++ RAILWAYS

J.C.GILLHAM FEB 87
409   BASED ON THE
ORDNANCE SURVEYS
OF 1906, 1912, & 1932
INF ALSO FROM AGG & AWB.
REVISED JAN 99

AW-AYRES WYND
BF-BRICK & FIRECLAY WKS
CH-COCKENZIE HOUSE
CS-CROWN SQUARE
EL-EAST LORIMER PLACE
FS-FRONT STREET
HH-HARLAW HILL
MS-MIDDLE STREET
MW-MILL WYND
RH-RAVENSHAUGH HOUSE
RR-REDBURN ROAD

✳ BUT THE 1900 ACT SPECIFIED ENTIRELY SINGLE TRACK, WITH 17 PASSING LOOPS WHERE MARKED ✳

GAUGE 4'-8½"
3·40 MILES DOUBLE TRK.
3·13 MILES SINGLE TRACK
6·53 MILES JOPPA TO P.S.

CROSSOVER ADDED APPROX HERE IN 1932

1923-28 ㉑ ㉒ 1932-46
MUSSELBURGH

HIGH ARCHED GATEWAY ADDED AFTER DEPOT OPENED, WITH FLAT AND SHIP SCALE ON BUTE ALONGSIDE IT

POWER STATION

TRAM DEPOT

ALL 3 INSETS
YARDS
0 25 50 100

ST. PETER'S CHURCH

NEWBIGGING

TOWN HALL

LEVENHALL
TERMINUS 1904-09

JOPPA
0 ⅛ ¼ ½ ¾ MILE 1

JOPPA TERMINUS

An early view. Edinburgh cable car awaits departure for Edinburgh Post Office while Musselburgh No. 6 is in the background. The notice on the poles describes the route it will take.
(Commercial card, courtesy A. W. Brotchie

Some twenty years later cable car 210 and ex-Sheffield No. 17 fulfil the same roles. The shelter was built in 1908.
(E. O. Catford, courtesy A. W. Brotchie

Finally on 23 June 1923 the tracks were joined. Edinburgh Corporation No. 56 is now on service 21 and Musselburgh No. 15 is freshly repainted for the new through service.
(E. O. Catford, courtesy A. W. Brotchie

FALKIRK 1 — ORIGINAL STOCK

No. 14 crossing the canal bridge at Camelon. *(Davidsons, Commercial card*

No. 12 in later years outside the depot at Larbert. *(NB Traction Collection*

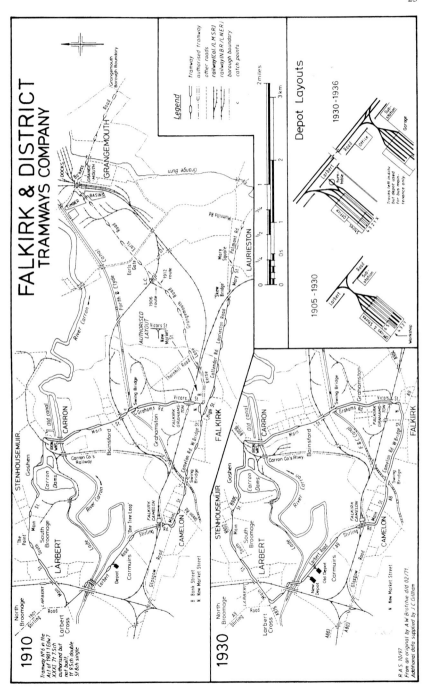

FALKIRK & DISTRICT TRAMWAYS COMPANY

Legend
- tramway
- authorised tramway
- other roads
- railway (Cal./LMSR)
- railway (NBR/LNER)
- borough boundary
- catch points

0   ¼   ½   ¾   1   2 miles
0   0.5   1   2   3 km

Depot Layouts

1905-1930

1930-1936

Tracks left in situ
but Depot used
for bus main-
tenance only

1910
Tramway No.6 in the
Act of 1901 1 Edw 7
XXXI 7r 7.5ch
authorised but
not built.
1f 9.5ch double
5f 6ch single

1930

R.A.S. 10/97
From an original by A.W. Brotchie dtd 02/71.
Additional data supplied by J.C. Gillham

FALKIRK 2 — MODERN STOCK

No. 17(ii), ex-Dearne District on Camelon swing bridge.
(Dr. H. Nicol, National Tramway Museum

No. 1(ii), new in 1929, lies disused in the depot yard in 1936.
(M. J. O'Connor, National Tramway Museum

No. 15(ii), is seen at the Plough, Stenhousemuir.
(National Tramway Museum

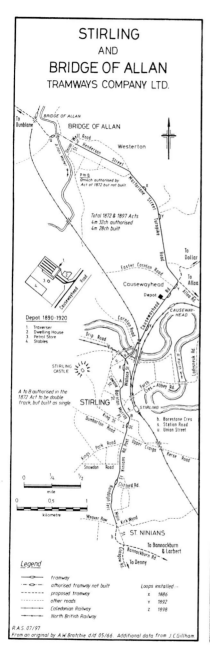

STIRLING
AND
BRIDGE OF ALLAN
TRAMWAYS COMPANY LTD.

BRIDGE OF ALLAN

BRIDGE OF ALLAN

To Dunblane

Westerton

P to q
0m4ch authorised by
Act of 1872 but not built

Total 1872 & 1897 Acts
4m 32ch authorised
4m 28ch built

To Dollar

Easter Cornton Road

To Alloa

Causewayhead
Depot

CAUSEWAYHEAD

Depot 1890-1920
1. Traverser
2. Dwelling House
3. Petrol Store
4. Stables

STIRLING
CASTLE

A to B authorised in the
1872 Act to be double
track, but built as single

STIRLING

STIRLING

b. Borestone Cres
s. Station Road
u. Union Street

Dumbarton Road

0   ¼   ½
mile

0   0.5   1
kilometre

ST. NINIANS

To Bannockburn
& Larbert

Bannockburn Rd

To Denny

Legend
— tramway
— authorised tramway not built
--- proposed tramway
--- other roads
Caledonian Railway
North British Railway

Loops installed:-
x   1886
Y   1892
Z   1898

R.A.S. 07/97
From an original by A.W. Brotchie d/d 05/66. Additional data from J.C. Gillham

ROUTE CONTRASTS
Above: Falkirk. Single line, a muddy road and no traffic.
Below: Wemyss. Private right-of-way and passing loop.   *(Both A. W. Brotchie Collection)*

STIRLING CONTRASTS

Three cars were purchased from the Edinburgh and District Tramways Co. in 1902. No. 24, rebuilt locally as a toastrack, is at the Bridge of Allan terminus ready to depart on its leisurely journey. *(NB Traction Collection*

No. 22, also ex-Edinburgh, was reconstructed and converted to petrol traction in 1913 and was in service until 1920. *(NB Traction Collection*

DUNFERMLINE CONTRASTS — 1

No. 27 heads cross country on the original single line and loop track outwards from
Dunfermline. *(A. W. Brotchie Collection*

No. 31 on the reserved tracks of the Rosyth line. *(A. W. Brotchie Collection*

30

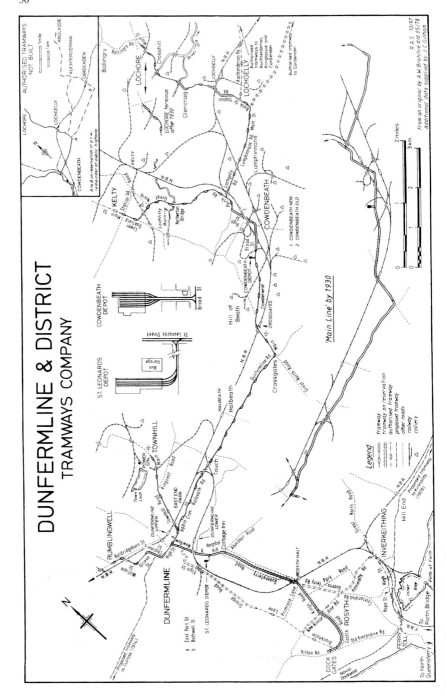

DUNFERMLINE & DISTRICT
TRAMWAYS COMPANY

DUNFERMLINE CONTRASTS — 2

No. 15 at the Lochore terminus on 13 August 1936 one year before closure.
(M. J. O'Connor, National Tramway Museum

No. 44, ex-Wemyss 19, photographed in Cowdenbeath depot yard, seated 45 passengers on upholstered seats, only ten fewer than the older cars with wooden seats. *(D. L. G. Hunter, courtesy A. W. Brotchie*

32

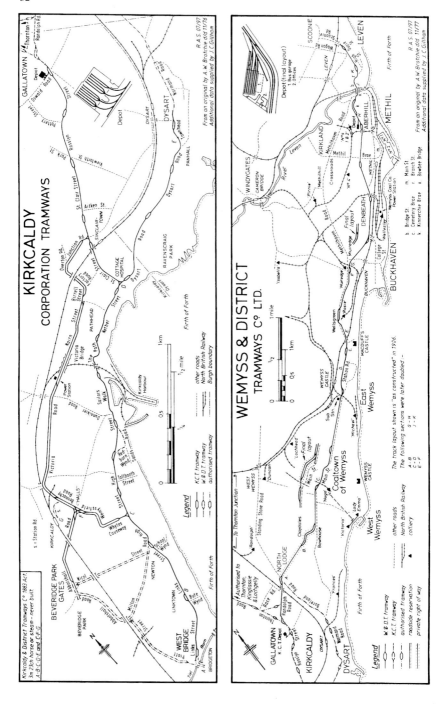

KIRKCALDY
CORPORATION TRAMWAYS

From an original by A.W. Brotchie dtd 11/76
Additional data supplied by J.C.Gillham

R.A.S. 07/97

Kirkcaldy & District Tramways C° 1883 Act.
3m 23ch horse or steam – never built.
A·B·C·D·E and C·F·G.

Legend

— ◯ — K.C.T. tramway
— ◯ — W.&D.T. tramway
— ◯ — authorised tramway

- - - - other roads
———————— North British Railway
———————— Burgh boundary

WEMYSS & DISTRICT
TRAMWAYS C° LTD.

From an original by A.W. Brotchie dtd 11/77
Additional data supplied by J.C.Gillham

R.A.S. 07/97

The track layout shown is "as constructed" in 1926.
The following sections were later doubled :-
A – B   G – H
C – D   J – K
E – F

Legend

— ◯ — W.&D.T. tramway
— ◯ — K.C.T. tramway
— ◯ — authorised tramway
·········· roadside reservation
———————— private right of way

- - - - other roads
———————— North British Railway
▲ colliery

b Bridge St.   m Main St.
c Cemetery Brae   r Branch St.
k Kinnerche Brae   x Bowbee Bridge

KIRKCALDY TRAMCARS

No. 11 in front of the red sandstone depot facade. *(National Tramway Museum*

No. 6 at Links terminus. The conductor is on the upper deck turning the trolley.
(Dr. H. A. Whitcombe, Science Museum, Science and Society Picture Library

WEMYSS TRAMCARS

Vestibuled No. 11 was delivered in 1906 from Brush of Loughborough.
(A. W. Brotchie Collection

No. 15 was one of four cars built by Milnes Voss of Birkenhead for miners traffic. These combination cars were later fully panelled as seen in this photograph.
(NB Traction Collection

TURN OF THE CENTURY TRACTION IN EDINBURGH

Edinburgh District horse tramcar No. 14 at Murrayfield terminus, possibly on its last journey. Note the cable tracks.   *(National Tramway Museum*

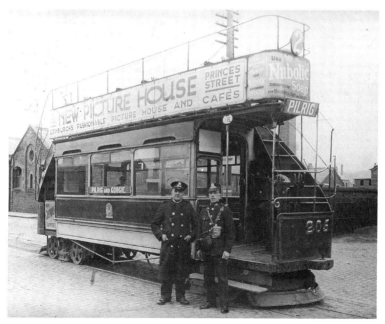

Cable tramcar No. 205, built by Brown Marshalls, is seen standing at Gorgie terminus, still in original condition.   *(A. W. Brotchie Collection*

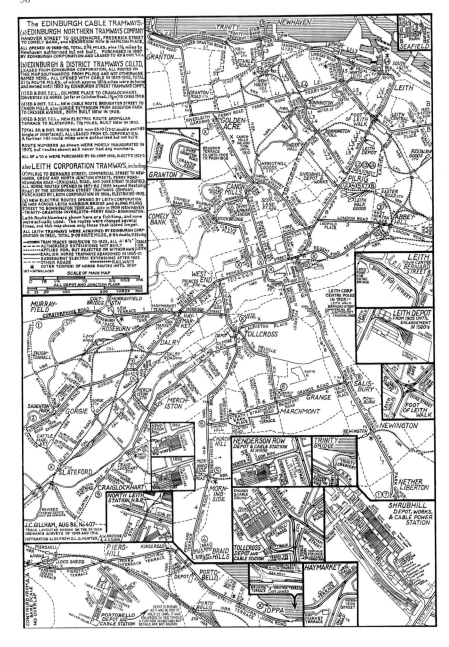

ELECTRIC TRACTION IN EDINBURGH

A fine view of the Scott Monument, Princes Street and the Edinburgh skyline, as Leeds Forge built No. 289 stands at the loading island.   *(E. O. Catford, courtesy A. W. Brotchie*

A posed view at Shrubhill depot with ex-cable cars No. 26 by Milnes and No. 169 by Brown Marshalls.   *(E. O. Catford, courtesy A. W. Brotchie*

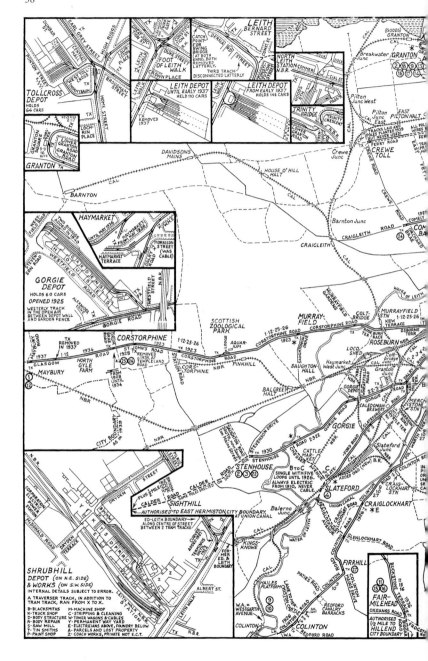

EDINBURGH
CITY CORPORATION
ELECTRIC TRAMWAYS

1922 TO 1956   4'-8½" GAUGE.

ROUTES AS ACQUIRED FROM LEITH
CORPORATION (NORTH OF LINE A-A-A)
IN NOVEMBER 1920, OR AS CONVERTED
FROM CABLE-CAR ROUTES IN 1922-23.

OUTER TERMINI IN
1922 ARE SHOWN ✱

EXTENSIONS OPENED
IN 1922-37 AS SHOWN.

MAXIMUM 46·44 MILES
(91·96 TRACK MILES)

ALL ABANDONED 1952-56

J.C.GILLHAM
FEB 86 - 408
REVISED OCT 97 WITH HELP
FROM A.G.GUNN & A.W.BROTCHIE
ALSO SEP 99

"MODERN" EDINBURGH TRAMCARS

Unusually all-steel car No. 262 by English Electric is seen on Service 17 to Granton on the former Leith system at Newhaven. Service 17 was normally worked by the older wooden cars.   *(M. J. O'Connor, National Tramway Museum*

Shrubhill built No. 67 was of the final Edinburgh design. Passengers alight at the Fords Road stop on Gorgie Road, before the car continues to Stenhouse. 8 August 1952. An authorised extension to Sighthill was never built.   *(R. J. S. Wiseman*

EDINBURGH CONTRASTS

Many Edinburgh streets were well suited to tramways as is evident at the junction of Leith Walk and London Road. No. 199 from Kings Road will be followed by No. 46 from Leith on 2 August 1953. *(R. J. S. Wiseman*

A tranquil scene with The Meadows in the background, as No. 40 climbs Marchmont Road at Warrender Park Terrace on 11 April 1955. *(R. J. S. Wiseman*

POPULAR DESTINATIONS

Portobello Swimming Pool and beach were popular in the Summer. Crowds at Kings Road queue for the trams back to the city on 2 August 1952. No. 45 on service 15 with No. 199, an extra, behind. *(R. J. S. Wiseman*

Edinburgh Zoo was also popular and an extra track was laid in for reversing trams at this point. 'Special' Ex-Manchester No. 411, operating on an enthusiasts tour, is sandwiched between Nos. 107 and 77 on 18 April 1954. *(R. J. S. Wiseman*

EDINBURGH JUNCTIONS

PRINCES STREET, EDINBURGH, FROM THE WEST END.

The West End of Princes Street is still a very busy junction. No. 63 from the Murrayfield direction is about to join the queue of cars in Princes Street. The Lothian Road tracks, to the right, lead to Tollcross. *(Commercial card*

The next major junction west was at Haymarket where the Dalry Road services diverged to the right. No. 310 is bound for Corstorphine on 3 July 1954, a year after the last trams ran to Slateford. *(R. J. S. Wiseman*

44

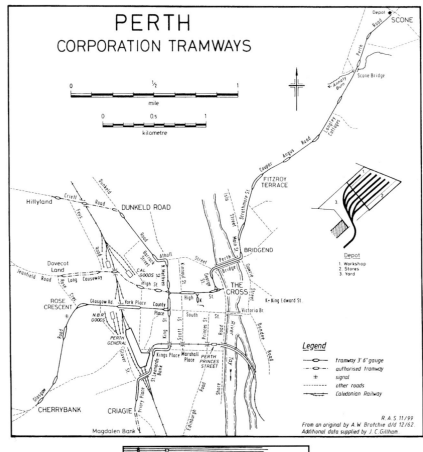

PERTH
CORPORATION TRAMWAYS

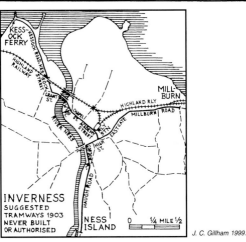

J. C. Gillham 1999.

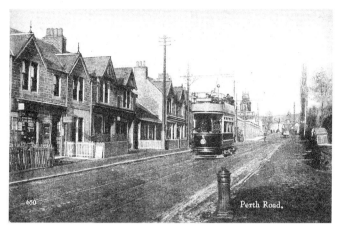

PERTH

The longest route was out along the Perth Road to Scone. No. 5 plies its lonely way along the single track.
(Commercial card courtesy NB Traction

Perth Road.

No. 11 at the Dunkeld Road terminus. The services to Dunkeld Road and Craigie terminated at The Cross.
(Courtesy NB Traction

East Bridge Street, Perth

No. 8 from Scone is at Bridge End and about to cross the bridge on its way to Cherrybank.
(Commercial card courtesy A. W. Brotchie

DUNDEE — TURN OF THE CENTURY TRACTION

Dundee District Reversible car No. 9 in the High Street in the 1890's.
(Courtesy NB Traction

Steam trailer No. 4 with engine No. 11 or 12 in the later days of steam operation as the overhead is already erected. *(Dundee City Council Central Library, Photographic Collection*

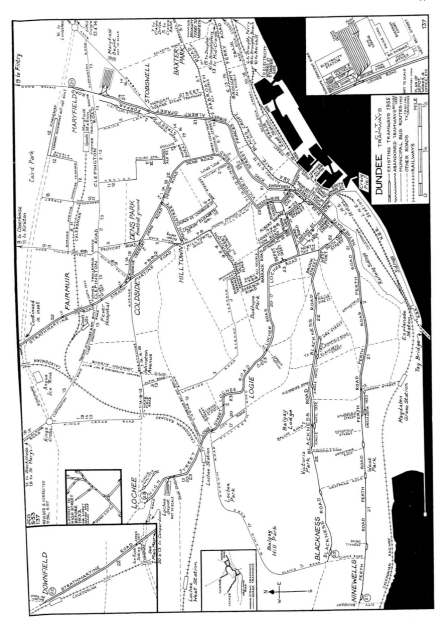

DUNDEE — ELECTRIC TRACTION

No. 50, was one of six combination cars built by Hurst Nelson for the Constitution Road line to Hilltown.
(NB Traction Collection

No. 99, the highest numbered Dundee tram, standing in the High Street.
(NB Traction Collection

No. 58, retained for football traffic, at the entrance to Maryfield depot.
(W. A. Camwell, National Tramway Museum

DUNDEE HIGH STREET

No. 7, for Downfield, is at the back of the queue of well filled cars. 2 August 1955.
(J. C. Gillham

Four months earlier things are quieter on the evening of 13 April 1955. No. 1 has loaded
passengers for Downfield while others wait by the tram stop. *(R. J. S. Wiseman*

DUNDEE VARIETY

Lochee car No. 26 inward bound at the junction of Lindsay Street and Nethergate. 6 August 1952.
(R. J. S. Wiseman

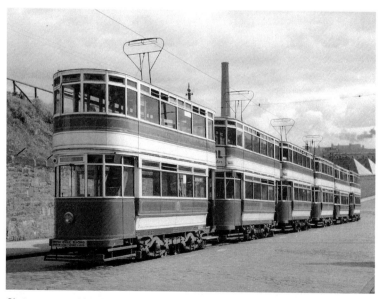

Six tramcars, waiting football traffic, in Provost Road siding. 4 September 1954.
(M. J. O'Connor, National Tramway Museum

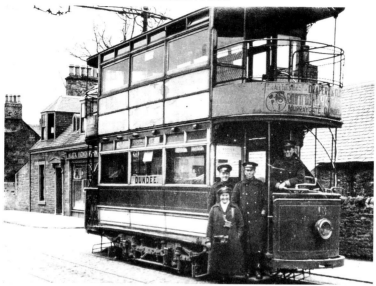

No. 13 with crew at Monifieth terminus. *(NB Traction Collection*

Ex-Dundee Corporation No. 15 was also photographed at Monifieth, in 1929.
(Dr. H. A. Whitcombe, Science Museum, Science & Society Picture Library

52

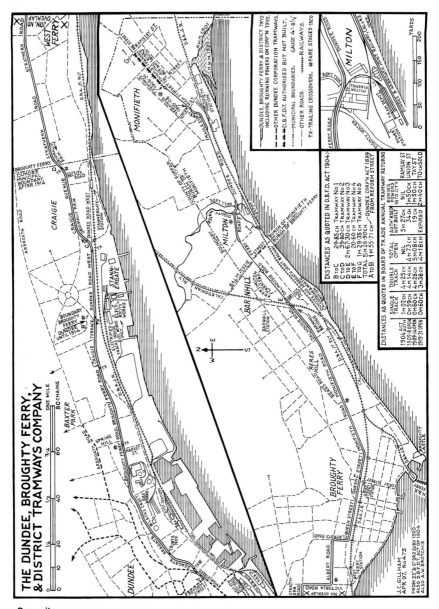

THE DUNDEE, BROUGHTY FERRY,
& DISTRICT TRAMWAYS COMPANY

Opposite:—
Horse tram of Starbuck design in King Street at Merkland Road. c1888-94.   *(NB Traction Collection*

Electric tramcars reached the Bridge of Dee on 2 June 1902. No. 5 is seen in Union Street early
in the Century.   *(Commercial card, Valentines Series*

No. 61 or 63 was converted back to horse car condition. This car is now back at King Street where
it was photographed on 3 August 1955.   *(J. C. Gillham*

ABERDEEN — TURN OF THE CENTURY TRACTION

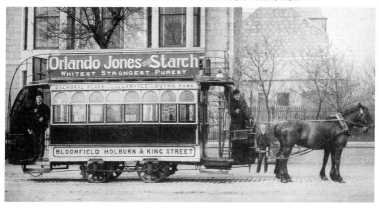

Union Street, Aberdeen   Valentine's Series

54

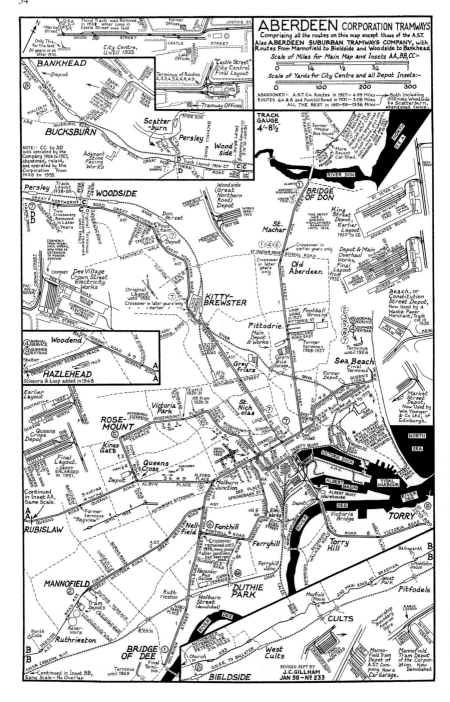

ABERDEEN CORPORATION TRAMWAYS

Comprising all the routes on this map except those of the A.S.T.
Also ABERDEEN SUBURBAN TRAMWAYS COMPANY, with
Routes From Mannofield to Bieldside and Woodside to Bankhead.

Scale of Miles for Main Map and Insets AA, BB, CC:-

Scale of Yards for City Centre and all Depot Insets:-

ABANDONED:- A.S.T. Co. Routes in 1927 – 4·59 Miles → Both Including
ROUTES 6A & 8 and Fonthill Road in 1931 – 3·08 Miles   0·52 miles Woodside
ALL THE REST in 1951-58 – 13·56 Miles   to Scatterburn,
abandoned twice.

TRACK GAUGE 4'-8½"

REVISED SEPT 97
J.C.GILLHAM
JAN 58 - Nº 233

ABERDEEN BALCONY TRAMCARS

The scene at Torry terminus shows No. 12 as rebuilt with long canopy and balcony top cover. Also converted for PAYE operation with reversed stairs, and fitted with folding windscreens. *(Aberdeen Transport Society*

The Woodside trams terminated in St. Nicholas Street. No. 34 is leaving for the intermediate Fountain crossover, while No. 67 inward bound is being followed by ex-Nottingham No. 18 on 14 June 1948. *(E. N. C. Haywood*

MAINTAINING ABERDEEN'S TRAMWAYS

No. 123, stands ready to depart at Mannofield. Note the tar boiler on left.
(W. A. Camwell, National Tramway Museum

Overhead repairs at Holburn Junction hold up No. 121 on 3 August 1952.
(R. J. S. Wiseman

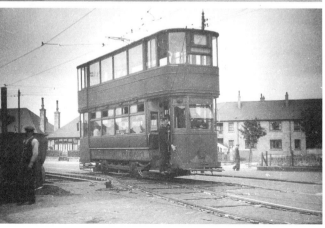

Track repairs in Great Northern Road on a wet August afternoon in 1947. Ex-Nottingham No. 12 on temporary track.
(R. J. S. Wiseman

57

TRAMS FROM MANCHESTER IN ABERDEEN

A contrast in styles and heights in Castle Street on 2 August 1952. Aberdeen built No. 92 dating from 1920 waits behind No. 52, ex-Manchester 502, built in 1930. Aberdeen raised the height of the roof of the Manchester cars. *(R. J. S. Wiseman*

No. 43, ex-Manchester 161, loads for Sea Beach at Holburn Junction on 4 August 1953.
(R. J. S. Wiseman

ABERDEEN'S MODERN TRAMCARS

Nos. 140 and 141, delivered in 1940, are seen in George Street at Fraser Place on 5 August 1953.
(R. J. S. Wiseman

No. 30, newly fitted with power operated centre-doors, in King Street works. 2 July 1954.
(E. N. C. Haywood

ABERDEEN SUBURBAN

A rather battered No. 2, bound for Bankhead is passing Bucksburn Fountain in the latter days of the system. *(Commercial card*

No. 11, the last tram purchased by the Company, at Bieldside terminus.
(National Tramway Museum

CRUDEN BAY

Tramcars Nos. 1 and 2 were three-window saloons built at Aberdeen. No. 2 was photographed in the late 1930's. *(W. A. Camwell, National Tramway Museum*

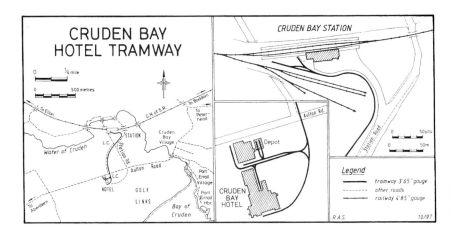

Maps of Edinburgh tramways, at 4¼ miles to the inch are available from J. C. Gillham at 209 Gunnersbury Park, Ealing, London W5. Prices:—horse £1, cable £1, electric £2. Also available:—Dundee, Aberdeen, and Broughty Ferry at £1 each, and Musselburgh at 50p.

TABLE SHOWING ROUTE AND TRACK LENGTHS

To be studied in conjunction with the Area Map on the inside of front cover

Undertaking	Traction	Gauge	FINAL MAXIMUM LENGTH OF ROUTE AS BUILT — SINGLE TRACK	DOUBLE TRACK	TOTAL	AUTHORISED BUT NOT BUILT	FIRST ROUTE STARTED	DURATION OF MAXIMUM MILEAGE OF TRACK (net route)	LAST ROUTE CLOSED OR SOLD	NOTES
EDINBURGH STREET TRAMW'S CO.	HORSE	4-8½	4-31	14-21	18-52		1871	1882-93	1904	A
ED. NORTHERN TRAMWAYS CO.	CABLE	DO	0-07	2-42	2-49	1-33	1888	1890-97	1897	B
EDINBURGH CORPORATION	HORSE	DO	2-50	12-75	15-45	6-58	1893	1893-99	1907	D
EDINBURGH CORPORATION	CABLE	DO	2-25	23-17	25-42	1-49	1899	1908-22	1923	D
EDINBURGH CORPORATION	ELEC	DO	0-74	46-26	47-20	3-28	1922	1938-52	1956	C
LEITH CORPORATION	HORSE	DO	1-78	3-11	5-09	0-69	1904	1904-05	1905	
LEITH CORPORATION	ELEC	DO	0-20	8-67	9-07	0-07	1905	1909-20	1920	E
MUSSELBURGH & DIST. E.L.&T. Cº LTD	ELEC	DO	3-10	3-32	6-42		1904	1925-28	1931	F
ED. SUBURBAN ELEC.TRYS.CO.(DALK./KEITH)	ELEC	DO	NIL	NIL	NIL	7-00	1906 ACT			G
COLINTON TRAMWAYS COMPANY	ELEC	DO	NIL	NIL	NIL	2-17	1909 ACT			H
ED.& QUEENSFERRY TRYS.,NAT.ELEC.	ELEC	DO	NIL	NIL	NIL	c11	1905 BILL			
ED. SUB'B'N ELEC.TRYS.SYNDC'T(QNS/FY)	ELEC	DO	NIL	NIL	NIL	c13	1905 PROPOSED			
ED. CORP'N 1918 TO QNSFY & PT.EDG.	ELEC	DO	NIL	NIL	NIL	c12	1918 BILL			
WINCHBURGH, OAKBANK OIL CO LTD	ELEC	DO				c3	1903	1903-61	1961	
FALKIRK & DISTRICT TRAMW'S CO.	ELEC	4-0"	5-11	2-53	7-64	4-34	1905	1910-23	1936	
STIRLING & BRIDGE OF ALLAN TRYS Cº LTD	HORSE	4-8½	4-10	0-18	4-28	0-04	1874	1898-17	1920	
DUNFERMLINE & DISTRICT TR'YS. CO.	ELEC	3-6"	5-20	13-13	18-33	12-05	1909	1930-30	1937	
KIRKCALDY & DISTRICT TRAMW'S CO.	STEAM	DO	NIL	NIL	NIL	3-23	1883 ACT			
KIRKCALDY CORPORATION	ELEC	DO	3-32	2-57	6-09	2-23	1903	1918-31	1931	
WEMYSS & DISTRICT TRAMWAYS Cº LTD	ELEC	DO	1-57	5-59	7-36	12-04	1906	1926-32	1932	J
PERTH & DISTRICT TRAMWAYS CºLTD	HORSE	DO	3-47	0-54	4-21	0-46	1895	1898-03	1905	
PERTH CORPORATION	ELEC	DO	3-07	1-74	5-01	1-33	1905	1910-28	1929	
ALMOND BANK BLEACH WORKS	ELEC	4-8½	c1		c1		1911		1962	
DALMUNZIE HOUSE	PET'L	2-6"	c2½		c2½		?	?	?	
INCHTURE (CALEDONIAN RLY)	HORSE	4-8½	c2		c2		1850	1870-99	1916	
DUNDEE & DISTRICT TRAMWAYS Cº LTD	HORSE STEAM	DO	3-20	4-00	7-20		1877	1895-99	1902	
DUNDEE CORPORATION TRAMS	ELEC	DO	2-64	13-61	16-45		1900	1925-27	1956	
DUNDEE CORP'N ELECTRICITY WORKS	ELEC	DO	0-64	0-09	0-73		1908	1908-61	1961	
DUNDEE BROUGHTY FERRY & DIST TRYS Cº LTD	ELEC	DO	0-60	4-28	5-08	0-19	1905	1908-14	1931	K
ABERDEEN DISTRICT TRAMWAYS CO	HORSE	DO	8-24	3-40	11-64		1874	1895-99	1902	
ABERDEEN CORPORATION TRAMS	ELEC	DO	0-69	15-63	16-52	2-18	1899	1928-30	1958	
ABERDEEN CORP'N GAS & ELEC WKS	STEAM BATTY	DO	c1¼		c1¼		1887	1925-69		
ABERDEEN SUBURBAN TRAMWAYS CO	ELEC	DO	4-05	0-42	4-47	3-21	1904	1904-27	1927	L
CULTER PAPER MILLS	ELEC	DO			?		1897	1897-20	1920	
STRABATHIE, SEATON BRICK,MURCARGOLF	STEAM PETRL	3-0"	c3		c3		1899	1899-24	1951	
CRUDEN BAY TR'Y, GT.NTH.SCOT.RLY	ELEC	3-6½	½	NIL	½		1899	1900-40	1940	
HOPEMAN TR'Y, SIR W.G.G.CUMMING	ELEC	4-8½	NIL	NIL	NIL	1-71	1901 ACT			M
INVERNESS, PROPOSED COMPANY		?	NIL	NIL	NIL	c3¼	1903 PROPOSED			

IMPORTANT:- All the above distances are quoted in MILES AND CHAINS, which was normal practice in the Tramway industry until approx 1920-30, or in Miles Furlongs & Chains.

NOTE:- 80 Chains = 8 Furlongs = 1 Mile. 1 chain = 22 yards. 10 chains = 1 furlong.

A, ED. STREET. The distances quoted are 1893 figures. Of the 18m52ch, 11m70ch were sold in 1893 to Ed. Corp and immediately leased to Dick Kerr & Co Ltd, 1m53ch (Portobello) were sold in 1896 to Ed. Corp., and 5m 09ch were sold in 1904 to Leith Corp.

B, ED. NORTHERN, Sold in 1897 to Ed.Corp. C, ED.ELEC, Including 9m07ex Leith & 2m76 exMuss.

D, ED. CORP HORSE & CABLE, Worked onLease 1894 to 1919 by Ed & Dist (D.K.), 1919-23 by Ed.Corp.

E, LEITH ELEC., Absorbed 1920 byEd.Corp. F, MUSS, 2m76ch Sold 1931 to Ed.Corp, the rest Abandnd.

G, ED. SUB. DALK., auth'd 5m29 single & 1m51double. H, COLINTON, auth 1m57sing & 0m40 doub, of which 1m41ch later built by Ed Corp. J, WEMYSS, Plus 2m 40ch Running Powers into Kirkcaldy.

K, BROUGHTY, Plus 1m50 R.P.into Dundee 1905-14, 2m40ch 1914-31. 70ch(of the5-08) sold to Dundee 1914.

L, AB'DN SUB, Plus 4m42ch RunningPowers intoCity. M, HOPEMAN, auth'd 1m69 single & 2ch double.

Tramcar Fleet Lists

All cars were four-wheel double-deck unless otherwise stated.

Seating figures shown 22/34 for lower and upper decks respectively.

The opening dates shown are the first day of regular public service.

The closing dates given for horse, steam or cable operating companies is the day the service closed, in most cases under another operator. For electric services it is the last full day of public service.

Aberdeen District Tramways Company

10.55 miles, 4ft. 8½in. gauge, horse traction, opened 31 August 1874, purchased by Aberdeen Corporation 27 August 1898. 39 open-top double-deck cars built by Starbuck or Shinnie of Aberdeen were transferred to the Corporation; one toastrack car built by the Company was not transferred. The Corporation built four toastrack cars and purchased seven double-deck cars from Liverpool Corporation. The cars were numbered in a separate series for each route. In 1878 sledges seating 20 passengers on knife-board seats, hauled by four horses, were used when snow and ice stopped normal operation. The last horse tram probably ran on 2 June 1902.

Aberdeen Corporation Tramways

15.78 miles, 4ft. 8½in. gauge, opened 23 December 1899, closed 3 May 1958. Livery green and cream with route colour 'bands'; black, blue, brown, dark green, red, white, and yellow, below the upper deck windows, until 1952.

Car Numbers	Type (as built)	Year Built	Builder	Seats	Truck(s)	Motors	Controllers
1-8 (a)	Open top Short canopy	1899	Brush	24/26	Brill 21E	Westinghouse 46 2 x 25hp	Westinghouse 90
9-20 (b)	Open top Short canopy	1901	Brush	24/28	Brill 21E	Westinghouse 46 2 x 25hp	Westinghouse 90
21-24 (c)	Open top Short canopy	1902	BEC	24/28	Brill 21E	Westinghouse 46 2 x 25hp	Westinghouse 90
25-56 (d)	Open top Short canopy	1902-3	BEC	24/28	Brill 21E	Westinghouse 46 2 x 25hp	Westinghouse 90
57-65 (e)	Open top Long canopy	1900-2	ACT	20/32	Brill 21E	Westinghouse 46 2 x 25hp	Westinghouse 90
66-69 (e)	Open top Short canopy	1900-2	ACT	20/28	Brill 21E	Westinghouse 46 2 x 25hp	Westinghouse 90
68-69(ii) 70-71(f)	Balcony	1912	Milnes Voss	24/36	Brill 21E	Westinghouse 46 2 x 25hp	Westinghouse 90
72-77 (g)	Balcony	1913	J. T. Clark Aberdeen	24/36	Brill 21E 2 x 30hp	Brush	Westinghouse 90M
78-83 (h)	Balcony	1914	Brush	24/36	M&G 21EM 2 x 30hp	Brush	Westinghouse 90M
84-86 (i)	Open top Long canopy	1918-9	ACT	18/36	Brill 21E 2 x 30hp	Brush	Westinghouse 90M
66-67(ii) (j)	Balcony	1919	ACT	24/36	Brill 21E 2 x 40hp	GE 200K	Westinghouse 90M
87-98 (j)	Balcony	1920-1	ACT	24/40	Brill 21E 2 x 35hp	Westinghouse 323	Westinghouse 90M
57-61(ii) (k)	Balcony	1922-3	ACT	24/36	Brill 21E 2 x 35hp	BTH GE200K	Westinghouse 90M
62-63(ii) (l)	Enclosed	1923	ACT	24/36	Brill 21E 2 x 35hp	BTH GE200K	Westinghouse 90M
99 (m)	Enclosed	1923	ACT	24/40	Brill 21E 2 x 40hp	GE 200K	Westinghouse 90M
100-105 (n, o)	Enclosed	1924-5	ACT	24/40	Peckham P35 2 x 40hp	GE 200K	BTH B510
106-115 (p)	Enclosed	1925	Brush	24/40	Peckham P35 2 x 40hp	BTH 506A	DK DB1 Form K3B
116-124 (o, q)	Enclosed	1926-31	ACT	24/40	Peckham P35 2 x 40hp	BTH 506A	DK DB1 Form K3B
126-137 (r)	Enclosed	1929	Brush	26/40	Peckham P35 2 x 50hp	DK 108C	DK DB1 Form K33B
1-18(ii) (s)	Enclosed	Bought 1936	EE	24/46	Peckham P22 2 x 40	GE 200K	DK DB1 Form K33B
138-139 (t)	Centre-entrance	1940	EE	30/44	EMB Lwt bogies 4 x 34hp	EE 327/1B	EE Z4 DB1
140-141	Enclosed	1940	EE	24/40	EMB Hornless 2 x 57hp	EE 305/1E	EE Z4 DB1
39-52(ii) (u)	Enclosed	Bought 1947-8	MCT	22/40	Peckham P35 2 x 50hp	MV105DW	EE DB1 or BTH510A
19-38(ii) (t)	Centre-entrance	1949	RYP	30/44	EMB Lwt bogies 4 x 34hp	EE 327/1B	EE Z6 DB1
(v)	Engineering car/van	1904	ACT	—	Brill 21E	?	Westinghouse
(w)	Snowbroom	1907	ACT	—	Brill 21E	?	Westinghouse

Aberdeen Corporation Tramways (continued)

Some or all cars in the series 1-83, except 21-24 and 57-69, were fitted with folding windscreens from 1912, and the majority adapted for PAYE fare collection from 1913; reverted to standard platform layout from 1921 onwards. Aberdeen experimented with new equipment over the years and exchanged equipments between cars. The equipment shown is that which is believed to have been installed at build; in some cases equipment was recovered from earlier cars.

Notes

(a) Initially numbered Woodside 1-8. Nos. 5-8 fitted with long canopies and - balcony top covers 1906, seating 24/32; Nos. 1-4 fitted with long canopies c1917, seating 24/32. No. 4 converted to salt car c1930, renumbered 4A in 1936.

(b) Initially numbered in separate route-number series. One car fitted for surface-contact current collection, 1901. No. 16 fitted in 1904 with extended top cover to the clerestory roof design of White, Great Grimsby Street Tramways. From 1904 all others rebuilt with long canopies and balcony top covers, seating 24/32. Nos. 12, 13, 20 converted to PAYE.

(c) Part of an order for 12 cars of which eight were rejected. Ordered with BEC trucks but probably on Brill 21E from new.

(d) No. 29 fitted with short-canopy top cover 1904, all others then rebuilt with long canopies and balcony top covers, seating 24/32. Converted to PAYE. From 1923 cars fitted with platform vestibules and later retrucked and re-equipped with DB1 K3 controllers and higher-powered motors. No. 56 converted to railgrinder and renumbered 4A(ii) in 1948.

(e) Rebuilt from horse cars and initially numbered in a separate route series. Nos. 66-69 to salt cars and snowploughs c1909. No. 61 or 63 reconverted to horse-car condition as '1' for 1924 jubilee of tramways. All others adapted as salt cars from 1920's.

(f) Converted to PAYE. Car platforms vestibuled 1923. Later retrucked with Peckham P35 and re-equipped with 40hp GE200K motors and DK DB1 K3 controllers.

(g) Built as PAYE cars; rebuilt as conventional with vestibuled platforms 1923. Nos. 72-73 retrucked with Peckham P35, others longer wheelbase Brill 21E, all re-equipped as note f above. No. 76 to salt car 1952; No. 73 bought for preservation in 1954, scrapped 1955 at Paisley.

(h) Built as PAYE cars; rebuilt as conventional with vestibuled platforms 1923. Later retrucked with Peckham P35, Nos. 81-83 later cascaded Brill 79E and 35hp GE 506A motors. Others re-equipped with 40hp GE200K motors and cascaded BTH B510 controllers.

(i) Brush motors and other components from earlier cars. Seating later 24/36. All to salt cars in 1932-3 and fitted with folding windscreens.

(j) Vestibuled from new. Later retrucked Peckham P35 and re-equipped as note f above.

(k) Vestibuled from new; totally enclosed 1936 seating 24/40. Retrucked Peckham P35.

(l) Retrucked with Peckham P35 and ultimately re-equipped with 50hp DK 108C motors and DK DB1 K3 controllers.

(m) Experimental high-speed tram. Retrucked and re-equipped as note l above.

(n) Later re-equipped with 50hp DK 108C motors and DK DB1 K3 controllers.

(o) Nos. 102 and 120 exchanged fleet numbers.

(p) All, except 109-110, re-equipped with 50hp DK 108C or DK 105C motors and DK DB1 K33 controllers. No. 106 possibly built at Aberdeen (with Brush parts?).

(q) Trucks were initially:—Nos. 116-119 79E; 120, 123, Peckham P35; 121-122 Brill 21E; 124 EMB Flexible axle. All laterly on Peckham P35. Nos. 116-122, 124 later re-equipped with 50hp DK 105C motors; No. 123 43hp CP motors. Nos. 123-4 with DK DB1 K33 controllers. No. 125 authorised but not built.

(r) An EMB Flexible-axle truck was tested under No. 129.

(s) Ex-Nottingham Corporation 181-199, built 1926. One car used for spares. Nos. 12, 14, 18 on Brill 21E trucks. Some cars had 40hp BTH 506 motors. Nottingham equipment was 40hp DK30B motors and EE DB1 K33B controllers so the cars were probably purchased without motors and Aberdeen stock used.

(t) Reseated 32/44 and power-operated platform doors fitted 1954-5.

(u) Ex-Manchester Pilcher 'Pullman' cars built 1930-32, Nos. 121, 493, 420, 671, 161, 610, 274, 669, 141, 270, 106, 225, 510, 502 respectively. Some cars had DK 105 50hp motors from Aberdeen stock.

(v) Known as emergency car from 1907. Dark blue livery.

(w) Rebuilt as a water car in 1908. 30hp motors.

Aberdeen Suburban Tramways Company

4.59 miles, 4ft. 8½in. gauge, opened 23 June 1904, closed, probably, week ending 9 July 1927. Livery vermillion and white.

Car numbers	Type (as built)	Year built	Builder	Seats	Truck(s)	Motors	Controllers
1-6	(Note a)	1904	Brush	22/35	Brush AA	GE 52-6T 2 x 25hp	BTH K10D
7-9	Balcony	1905	UEC	22/36	Brill 21E	GE 52-6T 2 x 25hp	BTH K10D
10	Balcony	1911	UEC	22/36	UEC Flexible axle	GE 52-6T 2 x 25hp	BTH K10D
11 (b)	Balcony	1914	UEC	22/36	UEC Flexible axle	GE 200K 2 x 40hp	BTH

Notes

(a) Nos. 1 and 5 open top, extended canopy, vestibuled; Nos. 2, 3, 4, 6, covered top with open balconies and three-compartment lower saloons, the central one being non-smoking. The roofs were later extended over the balconies. Saloons converted to normal layout 1910-11.

(b) Lower saloon of No. 11 now used as a trailer on the narrow gauge Alford Valley Railway.

Cruden Bay Hotel Tramway

0.66 miles, 3ft. 6½in. gauge, opened June 1899, closed to passengers 30 October 1932, to goods 31 December 1940 or possibly in March 1941. Livery purple lake, later green and cream, latterly varnished teak.

Car numbers	Type (as built)	Year built	Builder	Seats	Truck(s)	Motors	Controllers
1-2	Single-deck Combination	1899	GNSR Aberdeen	18	Peckham Cantilever Type 7B	? 1 x 15hp	Faceplate type

The tramway was owned by the Great North of Scotland Railway (GNSR) and passed to the London and North Eastern Railway in 1923. The stock also included a covered van for laundry and an open wagon for coal. A replica car is being reconstructed from Nos. 1 and 2 at the Grampian Transport Museum.

Dundee and District Tramway Company

7.25 miles, 4ft. 8½in. gauge, horse and steam traction, opened 30 August 1877, horse traction, 20 June 1885, steam traction. Purchased by Dundee Corporation 1 June 1899. Last horse tram June 1901, last steam tram 14 May 1902. Locomotives 1-13, Green 1885-94. Trailers: Nos. 1-4,7-8, 10-11, 14, 16-17, 21 and 23, double-deck, top-covered built by Milnes or by the Company. All were taken over by the Corporation and No. 21, now restored, is at the National Tramway Museum. Horse cars, Nos. 1-4, 7-13, 18-20 open top, knifeboard seats, Nos. 5, 6, 22, 24, garden seats, Nos. 14-15 single-deck, built locally or purchased from Glasgow and elsewhere. Nos. 5, 6, 9, 12-13, 18-20, 22-24 taken over by the Corporation.

Dundee Corporation Tramways

16.56 miles, 4ft. 8½in.gauge, opened 13 July 1900, closed 21 October 1956. Livery Indian red and cream, later leaf green and white.

Original Fleet

Car numbers	Type (as built)	Year built	Builder	Seats	Truck(s)	Motors	Controllers
1-10 (a)	Open top uncanopied	1900	ER&TCW	26/31	Brill 22E MxT bogie	DK 35A 2 x 35hp	DK DE1 Form B
11-20 (b)	Open top uncanopied	1900	ER&TCW	18/25	Brill 21E	DK 35A 2 x 35hp	DK DE1 Form E
21-40 (c)	Open top uncanopied	1900-1	ER&TCW	22/29	Brill 21E	DK 35A 2 x 35hp	DK DE1 Form B
41-48 (d)	Open top uncanopied	1902	Milnes	26/31	Brill 22E MxT bogies	DK 35A 2 x 35hp	DK DE1 Form B
49-54 (e)	Single-deck	1902	Hurst Nelson	42	Brill 27G bogies	DK 25A 4 x 25hp	DK QE1 Form A
55-60 (f)	Balcony	1907	Brush	22/36	Brill 21E	DK 3A4 2 x 36hp	DK DB1 Form C
61-66 (g)	Balcony	1908	Milnes Voss	22/36	Brill 21E	DK 3A4 2 x 36hp	DK DB1 Form C
69-72 (h)	Balcony	Bought 1914	Hurst Nelson	24/42	Hurst Nelson Swing-bolster	Siemens 250/19CT 2 x ? hp	Siemens
73-74 (h)	Balcony	Bought 1914	Hurst Nelson	24/42	Hurst Nelson Swing-bolster	DK 20A 2 x 40hp	DK DB1 Form K4
75-78 (i)	Balcony	1916	Hurst Nelson	22/36	Brill 21E	DK 20A 2 x 40hp	DK DB1 Form K4
67-68 (j)	Balcony	1920	Hurst Nelson	22/36	Brill 21E	DK 20A2 2 x 40hp	DK DB1 Form K4
79-82 (k)	Balcony	1920	Hurst Nelson	22/36	Brill 21E	DK 20A2 2 x 40hp	DK DB1 Form K4
83-90 (l)	Balcony	1921	Hurst Nelson	22/36	Brill 21E	DK 20A2 2 x 40hp	DK DB1 Form K4
91-94 (m)	Enclosed	1923-5	DCT	22/36	Brill 21E	DK 35A 2 x 35hp	DK DB1 Form K4
95 (n)	Enclosed	1925	DCT	22/36	Peckham P35	DK 35A 2 x 35hp	DK DB1 Form K4
96-99 (o)	Enclosed	1926	DCT	22/36	Peckham P35	DK 35A 2 x 35hp	DK DB1 Form K17B
19-28(ii) (p)	Enclosed	1930	Brush	28/34	EMB Flexible-axle	DK 105/1C 2 x 50hp	EE DK DB1 K17E
1	Water car	1901	ER&TCW	—	Brill 21E	DK 35A 2 x 35hp	DK DE1C Form A

Four steam locomotives, believed Nos. 2, 11, 12, 13, retained as snowploughs, were replaced in 1926 by electric cars Nos. 12, 17 and 20 cut down to single-deck. Replaced in their turn by Nos. 56 and 57, renumbered 1 and 2 in 1935, also cut down to single-deck. Two unpowered sand and salt wagons (Nos. 1 & 2) were supplied by Milnes Voss in 1909. Dundee Corporation also operated trolleybuses from 5 September 1912 until 13 May 1924.

Dundee Corporation Tramways (continued)

Notes

(a) Top covered 1907-10, seating 26/30. Rebuilt 1930-1 as enclosed.
(b) Top covered 1906-9; No. 16 with a new Hurst Nelson cover in 1916. Nos. 13 and 16 sold to Broughty Ferry Company in 1926.
(c) Top covered 1905-7, Nos. 21, 26, 36 having a low bridge design. Nos. 22-25, 27, 30, 35, 40 fitted with new Hurst Nelson top covers in 1915, seating 22/29. Nos. 21-28 re-numbered 33(ii), 37-39(ii), 67-68(iii), 69-70(ii) respectively in 1928-9.
(d) Top covered 1906-7, No. 43 low bridge. All fitted with Hurst Nelson canopy top-deck covers, seating 26/30; Nos. 44-46 in 1916; the remainder in 1925. Reconstructed enclosed and renumbered 11-18(ii) in 1927.
(e) Seating 30 in the central saloon and six in each open section. One outside seat later removed to give a total of 41.
(f) Nos. 57, 59 low bridge cars; No. 58 had top cover removed later.
(g) No. 65 had top cover removed later Nos. 61, 62, 64, 66 fitted 35hp DK 35A motors. Nos. 61-63 renumbered 52(ii), 58(ii) and 59(ii) respectively in 1936.
(h) Ex-Paisley & District Tramways Nos. 53-58 built 1910-11. Nos. 73-74 renumbered 67-68(ii) in 1927. No. 68(ii) fitted Brill 21E truck in 1929.
(i) Nos. 77-78 renumbered 73-74(ii) respectively in 1927. Nos. 73-74(ii) & 75-76 renumbered 47-50(iii) in 1936.
(j) Renumbered 41-42(ii) in 1928. The original 67-68 were two single-deck Railless trolleybuses with Milnes Voss bodies bought in 1912. Sold to Halifax in 1917 but never used.
(k) Renumbered 43-46(ii) in 1928.
(l) Renumbered 47-54(ii) in 1928 and again in 1936 to 34-36(ii), 37-39(iii), 40(ii) and 51(iii).
(m) Renumbered 77-80(ii) in 1928 and 53-54(iii), 55-56(ii) in 1936.
(n) Fitted with 50hp DK 108/1C motors in 1929; renumbered 81(ii) in 1928 and 29(ii) in 1936.
(o) Fitted with 50hp DK 108/1C motors in 1929; renumbered 82-85(ii) in 1928, and 30-33(ii) in 1936.
(p) "Lochee" cars. Long wheelbase, 8ft. 6in. trucks.

Fleet in 1950 as rebuilt

Car numbers	Original numbers	Date rebuilt	Seats	Truck(s)	Motors	Controllers
1-10	1-10	1930-1	26/40	EMB	EE DK 105/1C	EE DK DB1
				Flexible axle	2 x 50hp	Form K 17C
11-18 (q)	41-48	1928-30	26/40	EMB 79EX	EE DK 105/1C 2 x 50hp	EE DK DB1 Form K 17C
19-28	19-28	—	28/34	EMB	EE DK 105/1C	EE DK DB1
				Flexible axle	2 x 50hp	Form K 33E
29-33 (r)	95-99	—	22/36	Peckham P35	EE DK 108/1C 2 x 50hp	EE DK DB1 Form K 17B
34-40	83-89	1932	22/34	EMB	EE DK 105/1C	DK DB1
				Flexible axle	2 x 50hp	Form K 17E
41-46	67-68 79-82	1932-3	22/34	EMB Flexible axle	EE DK 105/1C 2 x 50hp	DK DB1 Form K4
47-48	77-78	1932	22/34	EMB	EE DK 105/1C	DK DB1
				Flexible axle	2 x 50hp	Form K4
49-50	75-76	1932	22/34	EMB Flexible axle	EE DK 105/1C 2 x 50hp	BTH B 510
51 (s)	90	1932	22/34	EMB Swing axle	EE DK 105/1C 2 x 50hp	DK DB1
52 (t)	61	1933	22/36	EMB Hornless	EE DK 105/1C 2 x 50hp	DK DB1 Form K4
53-56 (t)	91-94	—	22/36	EMB Swing axle	DK 20A 2 x 40hp	EE DK DB1 Form 17E
1-2	56-57	1935 to Single-deck	—	Brill 21E	DK 20A 2 x 40hp	DK DB1

Notes

(q) Nos. 11-12 (ex 41-42) initially fitted Peckham P35 trucks.
(r) No. 29 (ex-95) had a DB1 Form K4 controller.
(s) Initially EMB Hornless truck and DK 20A2 40hp motors.
(t) In 1953 some motors were replaced by EE 305's ex-Sunderland.

Dundee, Broughty Ferry and District Tramways Co. Ltd.

5.10 miles, 4ft. 8½in. gauge, opened 27 November 1905, closed 15 May 1931. Livery lake and cream.

Car numbers	Type (as built)	Year built	Builder	Seats	Truck(s)	Motors	Controllers
1-12 (a)	Open top uncanopied	1905	Brush	22/29	Brush AA	GE 53-3T 2 x 37hp	GE K10
13-14	Balcony	1907	Brush	22/36	Brush AA	GE 53-3T 2 x 37hp	GE K10
15-16 (b)	Top cover uncanopied	Bought 1926	ER&TCW	18/26	Brill 21E	DK 35A 2 x 35hp	DK DE1 Form B

Notes

(a) Nos. 1 & 2 fitted with Hurst Nelson top covers in 1909.
(b) Ex-Dundee City Tramways Nos. 13 & 16 built 1900.

66

Dunfermline and District Tramways Company

18.41 miles, 3ft. 6in.gauge, opened 2 November 1909, closed 4 July 1937. Livery green and cream.

Car numbers	Type (as built)	Year built	Builder	Seats	Truck(s)	Motors	Controllers
1-20	Open top	1909	UEC	22/34	Brill 21E	BTH GE58-4T 2 x 37hp	BTH K10D
21-24	Open top	1910	UEC	22/34	Brill 21E	BTH GE58-4T 2 x 37hp	BTH K10D
25-28	Open top	1912	UEC	22/34	Brill 21E	BTH GE58-4T 2 x 37hp	BTH K10D
29-43	Open top	1917	UEC	22/34	UEC	GE 249A 2 x 37hp	DK DB 1B
44-45 (b)	Open top	Bought 1919	ER&TCW	22/26	Brill 21E	DK 25B 2 x 27hp	DK DB 1B
44-45(ii) (c)	Single-deck	Bought 1932	Brush	45	M&G EqW bogies	BTH 249AA 2 x 37hp	BTH B18

Notes

(a) No. 34, cut down to single-deck, was sold to the Giants Causeway tramway; also one other which was not used.
(b) Ex-Ilkeston Corporation via Notts & Derbys Traction Company. Believed to be from the series 1-9, built 1902.
(c) Ex-Wemyss & District Tramways Company Nos. 19 and 18, built 1925.

Edinburgh Street Tramways Company

18.65 miles, 4ft. 8½in. gauge, horse traction, opened 6 November 1861. Maximum 84 open-top cars with route colour liveries. Most sold in 1893 to Dick Kerr, thence in 1894 to the Edinburgh and District Tramways Company. Others retained for use in Leith. Two Kitson tram engines, built in 1881-2, were used experimentally on the Portobello line. Horse cars in Edinburgh replaced by cable cars from 1899 onwards. Last horse car 24 August 1907. Horse cars in Leith replaced by electric cars; last horse car 2 November 1905.

Edinburgh Northern Tramways Company

2.61 miles, 4ft. 8½in. gauge, cable traction, opened 28 January 1888, operated by Edinburgh District from 1 January 1897, officially transferred 1 July 1897. Livery dark blue and cream.

Cable car numbers	Type (as built)	Year built	Builder	Seats	Truck(s)
1-8	Open top Reversed stair	1887	Metropolitan	20/36	Outside frame bogies
9-16	Open top Normal stair	1890	Falcon	18/22	Outside frame bogies
17-18 (a)	Single-deck	1894-5	?	26	?

Notes

(a) Supposedly American built.

Edinburgh and District Tramways Co. Ltd.

25.52 miles, 4ft.8½in. horse and cable traction. Operated from 1894 all lines ex-EST Co., and from 1897 the cable tramways ex-ENT Co. All lines, except Craiglockhart were converted to cable traction 1899-1901. Last horse tram 24 August 1907 when Craiglockhart converted to cable traction. 18 horse cars were retained in case of cable breakdown. Probably Nos. 75-76, 84, 86-7, 90, 92-3, 95-9, 102, 108, 110 and 170-1, the last two added in 1899. These numbers were never allocated to cable cars. Electric operation introduced on the Slateford route 8 June 1910. Livery madder and cream.

Cable car numbers	Type (as built)	Year built	Builder	Seats	Truck(s)
121-128	Open top	1887	Metropolitan	20/32	Outside frame bogies (ex-ENT)
129-136	Open top	1890	Falcon	18/22	Outside frame bogies (ex-ENT)
137-138 (a)	Single-deck	1894-5	?	26	? (ex-ENT)
112 (b)	Open top	1897	E&DT	18/28	Inside frame bogies
139-144	Open top	1897	Milnes	18/22	Inside frame bogies
25 cars (c)	Open top	1898	Milnes	20/28	Inside frame bogies
120 cars (d)	Open top	1898-9	Brown Marshall	20/28	Inside frame bogies
209-228 (e)	Open top	1903	ER&TCW	20/28	Pressed steel bogies
5 cars (f)	Open top	1901-8	E&DT	18/28	Inside frame bogies
16 cars (g)	Balcony	1906-11	E&DT	20/28	Inside frame bogies
4 cars (h)	Open top	1910	Milnes	20/28	Brill 22E bogies

67

Edinburgh District Tramways Co. Ltd. (continued)

Notes

(a) Renumbered 7 and 13 c1901.
(b) Prototype car.
(c) Believed Nos. 1, 26, 28, 38-40, 45-46, 55, 62-5, 67-8, 73-4, 79, 81-3, 94, 103-5. All top-covered 1908-12 except Nos. 28, 38, 64, 74.
(d) Nos. 2-4, 6, 8-12, 14, 16, 18, 20-4, 29-34, 36, 41-4, 56-8, 60-1, 69-71, 77-8, 80, 85, 88-9, 91, 100-1, 106-7, 109, 111, 114-20, 137-8, 145-69, 172-208. Nos. 12, 24, 111, 137, 151-2, 206, top-covered 1912.
(e) Top-covered 1907.
(f) 5 cars Nos. 15, 17, 19, 53, 113 rebuilt from horse cars.
(g) 16 cars. Nos. 5, 13(ii), 25, 27, 35, 37, 47-52, 54, 59, 66, 72. Nos. 25, 27 built as open-top, covers added 1907.
(h) Nos. 28, 38, 64, 74 (see note c) fitted with DK 9A2 motors and DK DB1 Form K3 controllers for the new Slateford electric route.

Edinburgh Corporation Tramways

47.24 miles, 4ft. 8½in. gauge, operated cable and electric traction from 1 July 1919, cable traction closed 23 June 1923, electric traction 16 November 1956. Livery madder and white (window pillars brown). The Corporation took over 209 cable cars (Nos.1-228 with gaps) and four electric cars. A further 37 electric cars and one water car were taken over with the Leith Corporation Tramways on 2 November 1920.

Cable cars converted by Edinburgh Corporation to electric operation.

1. Open-top cars converted to open-top electric cars: Nos. 18, 24, 42, 57, 60, 69, 77, 88, 106-7, 112, 119, 145-6, 153, 161-2, 166-7, 176-7, 179-181, 188, 190, 196, 200, 204-5.
2. Open-top cars converted to covered-top electric cars with new balcony covers by Hurst Nelson and other builders. Nos. 2-4, 6, 8-11, 14, 16, 20-23, 29-34, 36, 41, 44, 56, 58, 61, 70-1, 78, 80, 85, 89, 91, 100-1, 109, 114-8, 120, 138, 147-50, 154-60, 163-5, 168-9, 172-5, 178, 182-7, 189, 191-5, 197-9, 201-3, 207-8. Seating 20/36.
3. Balcony cable cars converted to balcony electric cars: Nos. 1, 5, 12, 13 (former 13(ii) in EDT fleet), 25-7, 35, 37, 39-40, 45-52, 54-55, 59, 62-63, 65-68, 72-73, 79, 81-3, 94, 103-5, 111, 137, 151-2, 206, 209-228. Seating 22/36; No. 222 rebuilt enclosed seating 20/42. Nos. 5, 13, 25-7 renumbered 76(ii), 169(ii), 172(ii), 112(ii) and 73(ii) respectively.
4. "Slateford" bogie electric cars (ex-cable) Nos. 28, 38, 64, 74 converted to single-truck balcony cars; later renumbered 229, 230, 268, 269 respectively.
5. Ex-Edinburgh Northern cable cars Nos. 123, 125, and two others, converted to open-top electric cars and renumbered Nos. 75, 76, 84, 86.

Wooden-bodied electric cars, acquired or built 1921-34.

Car numbers	Type (as built)	Year built	Builder	Seats	Truck(s)	Motors	Controllers
229-230 (a)	Balcony	1898	Milnes	20/28	Brill 22E bogies	DK 9A2 2 x 40hp	DK DB1 Form K3
231-245 (b)	Balcony	1905	UEC	22/36	Brill 21E	GE 54 2 x 25hp	BTH B18
246-249 (b)	Balcony	1905	Brush	22/32	Brush AA	Brush 1002B 2 x 25hp	Brush 3A
250-260 (b)	Open top	1905	Brush	22/34	Brush AA	Brush 1002B 2 x 25hp	Brush 3A
261-263 (b)	Balcony	1905	UEC	22/34	Brill 21E	GE 54 2 x 25hp	BTH B18
264-266 (b)	Balcony	1905	Brush	22/32	Brush AA	Brush 1002B 2 x 25hp	Brush 3A
267 (b)	Balcony	1906	Brush	22/34	Brush AA	GE 54 2 x 25hp	BTH B18
121-136(ii) (c)	Balcony	1922	McHardy & Elliot	22/34	Peckham P22	MV 101 2 x 40hp	EE DB1 Form K7B
268-269 (a)	Balcony	1898	E&DT	20/28	Brill 22E bogies	DK 9A2 2 x 40hp	DK DB1 Form K3
270-311 (d)	Balcony	1923	Leeds Forge (Bristol)	20/36	Peckham P22(HN)	MV 101 2 x 40hp	EE DB1 Form K7B
14 cars (e)	Balcony	1923	Leeds Forge (Bristol)	20/36	Peckham P22(HN)	MV 101 2 x 40hp	EE DB1 Form K7B
312-331 (d)	Balcony	1924	EE	20/36	Peckham P22(HN)	MV 101 2 x 40hp	EE DB1 Form K7B
332-342 (d)	Balcony	1925	ECT	20/36	Peckham P22(HN)	MV 101 2 x 40hp	BTH B510
343-353 (d)	Balcony	1926	ECT	20/36	Peckham P22(HN)	MV 101 2 x 40hp	BTH B510
14 cars (f)	Balcony	1924-5	ECT	20/36	Peckham P22	MV 101 2 x 40hp	BTH B510
354-366 (d)	Balcony	1929	ECT	20/36	Peckham P22	DK 94 2 x 50hp	BTH B510
38 cars (g)(h)	Balcony	1926-9	ECT	20/36	Peckham P22	DK94 2 x 50hp	BTH B510

Edinburgh Corporation Tramways (continued)

Car numbers	Type (as built)	Year built	Builder	Seats	Truck(s)	Motors	Controllers
367-370	Enclosed	1929-30	ECT	20/38	Peckham P22	MV 101B 2 x 50hp	BTH B510
9 cars (i)	Enclosed	1929-31	ECT	20/38	Peckham P22	MV 101B 2 x 50hp	BTH B510
38 cars (j)(h)	Enclosed	1929-34	ECT	20/36	Peckham P22	MV 101B 2 x 50hp	BTH B510

Electric cars built or acquired 1932-1950

Car numbers	Type (as built)	Year built	Builder	Seats	Truck(s)	Motors	Controllers
250-259(ii) (k)	Enclosed	1932-3	RYP	20/36	M&T Swing-link	MV 101B 2 x 50hp	BTH B510
180(ii) (l)	Enclosed Alloy-frame	1932	ECT	26/38	EMB Flexible axle	MV 101B 2 x 50hp	MV OK39B
260, 265(ii) (m)	Enclosed All-steel	1933	MC	24/40	M&T Swing-link	MV 101B 2 x 50hp	BTH B510E
261(ii) (m)	Enclosed mainly steel	1933	ECT	24/36	Peckham P22	MV 101 2 x 40hp	BTH B510E
231, 239 240(ii)	Steel body, domed roof	1934	HN	24/36	M&T Swing-link	MV 101B 2 x 50hp	BTH B510E
6 cars (n)	Steel body domed roof	1934	MC	24/38	M&T Swing-link	MV 101B 2 x 50hp	BTH B510E
3 cars (o)	Steel body	1934	EE	24/34	M&T Swing-link	MV 101B 2 x 50hp	BTH B510E
11-18(ii) (p)	Steel body sloping ends	1935	HN	24/34	Peckham P22	MV 101B 2 x 50hp	BTH B510E
6 cars (q)	Steel body sloping ends	1935	EE	24/34	Peckham P22	MV 101B 2 x 50hp	BTH B510E
6 cars (r)	Steel body sloping ends	1935	MC	24/34	M&T Swing-link	MV 101B 2 x 50hp	BTH B510E
46 cars (s)	Enclosed domed roof	1934-7	ECT	24/38	Peckham P22	MV 101B 2 x 50hp	BTH B510E
38 cars (t)	Enclosed domed roof	1938-1950	ECT	24/38	Peckham P22	MV 101B 2 x 50hp	BTH B510E
401-411 (u)	Enclosed	Bought 1946-8	MCT	22/40	Peckham P35	MV 105 2 x 50hp	BTH B510

Works cars

Car numbers	Type (as built)	Year built	Builder	Seats	Truck(s)	Motors	Controllers
1 (v)	Grinding car	1905	UEC	—	Peckham	GE 58	BTH B18
2 (w)	Welding car	1898	Brown Marshalls	—	Peckham	MV 101?	?
3 (x)	Grinder car	c1901	E&DT	—	Peckham	MV 101?	?
4-10 (y)	Salt cars	1897-1901	Various	—	Brill 21E or Brush AA	MV 101?	?
3 (z)	Trackwork	c1910	E&DT	—	Peckham	MV 101	?

Notes

Edinburgh tried various sample motors and equipments from 1921 onwards. Motors included MV 102, MV 323, GE 200K, DK 34A, DK 94/1A and BTH 265 designed for use with 30in.-40in. wheels; MV101, 101B and 105 motors were designed for the newer 24in.-27in. wheels. Many MV 101B motors were fitted with roller bearings and became MV 101BR. DK DB1-K7B controllers had "double electric braking".

(a) Former cable cars 28, 38, 64, 74 respectively, No. 229 retrucked Peckham P22, 1922, others Brill 21E or Brush at the same time. No. 268 renumbered 23(ii), later 41(ii).

(b) Ex-Leith Nos. 1-37 in sequence. 34 cars received BTH B510 controllers from 1923 onwards, also Nos. 232-3, 243, 247-8 fitted Peckham P22 trucks.

(c) Top decks built by Hurst Nelson, end balconies enclosed circa 1930-3.

(d) End balconies enclosed circa. 1930-3.

(e) 14 cars Nos. 87, 90, 92-3, 95-9, 102, 108, 110, 170-1. See also notes d.

(f) 14 cars numbered cars, Nos. 7, 28, 38, 43, 53, 64, 74, 113, 139-142, in 1924; Nos. 143-4 in 1925. In 1935 Nos. 7, 28, renumbered 86(ii), 151(ii) respectively. See also note d.

(g) 38 replacement cars, No. 36 in 1926, Nos. 3, 33, 114, 117, 147, 178, 183, 185, 187, 192, 208 in 1927, Nos. 18, 20, 24, 42, 57-8, 77, 106, 115, 153-4, 174, 176, 179, 188, 194, 196, 200, 205 in 1928; Nos. 60, 79, 146, 181, 268 in 1929. Nos. 101, 198 in 1930. Nos. 3, 18, 20, 24, renumbered 75(ii), 182(ii), 184(ii), 78(ii) in 1935.

(h) Replacements for cable cars with the same numbers and re-using the same top decks where available.

(i) 8 replacement cars. Nos. 107, 162, in 1930; Nos. 119, 161, 166-7, 177, 264 in 1931; Nos. 177 and 264 on EMB trucks, 1932-3; 264 later on M&T Swinglink truck with MV OK35B controllers. Also a new car, No. 371, it had an EMB Hornless truck and MV 107 75hp motors, renumbered 266(ii) in c1933.

(j) 38 replacement cars. Nos. 70 in 1929, Nos. 31, 104, 116, 155, 163, 168, 201, in 1930; Nos. 118, 149, 156, 158, 207 in 1931; Nos. 16, 44, 46, 65, 68, 85, 109 in 1932; Nos. 6, 29, 34, 80-1, 89, 100, 186, 193, 197, 203, 206, in 1933; Nos. 94, 148, 152, 159, 175, 191, in 1934. In 1935 Nos. 6, 16, 29 renumbered 84(iii) 61(ii), 138(ii) respectively. See also note h.

Edinburgh Corporation Tramways (continued)

(k) No. 256 was initially fitted with an EE FL32 type truck which was transferred to No. 267 when new in 1934.
(l) Experimental modern car, bright red livery until 1935. EMB truck was replaced by M&T Swing-link in 1932 after a few days in service.
(m) Experimental cars.
(n) 6 cars Nos. 241-2, 244-6, 249(ii). The latter initially had platform doors.
(o) Three cars, Nos. 262, 263, 267(ii). No. 267 had the EE FL 32 truck initially, later Peckham P22.
(p) HN parts supplied for assembly in Edinburgh. Nos. 11-2,(ii), 16(ii) later M&T Swing-link trucks. No. 13 was third car with this number.
(q) 6 replacement cars Nos. 19(ii), 20(iii), 21-22(ii), 23-24(iii). Nos. 21-24 later on EMB hornless trucks.
(r) 6 replacement cars, Nos. 25-28(ii), 29(iii), 30(ii).
(s) 46 replacement cars, No. 69 in 1934, Nos. 32, 55-56, 62, 67, 71, 83, 88, 103, 105, 111, 112(iii), 137, 145, 150, 157, 160, 164-5, 189, 190, 202, 204, 229-30, 269 in 1935; 41(iii), 45, 120, 173, 195, 199, 232-7, in 1936; Nos. 40, 82, 91, 238, 243, 247-8 in 1937. Built ECT on EMB hornless trucks.
(t) 38 replacement cars, Nos. 39, 63, 76(iii), 218, 226 in 1938; Nos. 52, 215-6, 220-3, 227 in 1939; Nos. 54, 212, 214 in 1940; Nos. 72, 211 in 1941; No. 213 in 1942; No. 209 in 1943; No. 51 in 1945; Nos. 47, 66 in 1946; Nos. 59, 73(iii), 210, 217, 224 in 1947; Nos. 35, 219, 228, in 1948; No. 37 in 1949 and Nos. 48-50, 169(iii), 172(iii), 225 in 1950. ECT built on HN underframes. No. 35 now preserved, presently (1998) at Crich.
(u) Ex-Manchester "Pilcher" Pullman cars built 1930-2, Manchester Nos. 173, 676, 196, 125, 558, 217, 389, 231, 242, 349, 381 respectively. Trucks altered by ECT to, or replaced by, P22 type. In 1950-4 some MCT trucks were exchanged with Peckham P22 trucks from withdrawn cars.
(v) Ex-Leith No. 60.   (w) Ex-Edinburgh & District No. 177.   (x) Ex-rebuilt horse car No. 17.
(y) Ex-Nos. 15, 19, 75, 76, 84, 86,112.   (z) Initially numbered 10. Ex-No. 51.
No. 226 is now, (1999) under restoration in Edinburgh. The lower saloons of Nos. 16, 49, 79 and 115 also still exist.

Falkirk and District Tramways Company

7.80 miles, 4ft. 0in. gauge, opened 21 October 1905, closed 21 July 1936. Livery Prussian blue and cream, later red and cream.

Car numbers	Type (as built)	Year built	Builder	Seats	Truck(s)	Motors	Controllers
1-15 (a)	Open top	1905	CG de C	22/26	Arbel	Ganz 2 x 30hp	Bruce Peebles PPP
16-18 (b)	Open top	1905	Brush	22/28	Brush AA	Ganz 2 x 30hp	Bruce Peebles PPP
19 (c)	Water car	1908	M&G	—	M&G 21EM	BTH GE58-4T 2 x 37hp	BTH B18
1-10(ii) (d)	Single-deck	1929-30	Brush	30	Brush Burnley bogies	BTH 265S 2 x 35hp	BTH B510
13-16(ii) (e)	Single-deck	1931	Brush	28	Brush Burnley bogies	BTH 265S 2 x 35hp	BTH B510
11-12(ii) (f)	Single-deck	Bought 1933	EE	27	Peckham P22	EE DK30B 2 x 40hp	EE DB1 Form K3B
17-19(ii) (f)	Single-deck	Bought 1933	EE	27	Peckham P22	EE DK30B 2 x 40hp	EE DB1 Form K3B

Notes
(a) Built in France at St. Denis by the Compagnie Générale de Construction. Motors supplied by Bruce Peebles. Original trucks replaced in 1908 by solid forged 21E type built by Hurst Nelson; also new 30hp BTH GE58-4T motors and BTH B18 controllers.
(b) Fitted 1908 with Hurst Nelson top covers.
(c) General works vehicle with rectangular tank, livery brown.
(d) BTH 265S motors were worm drive.
(e) Seating for 26 in the saloon plus two on the platform without resistances fitted. No. 14(ii) has been restored on HN bogies ex-Glasgow Subway with 60hp MV 101 DR motors, and is now preserved at Grangemouth.
(f) Ex-Dearne District Light Railways. Built 1924, shortened on arrival and did not enter service until 1934. No. 19 had longitudinal seating for 26.

Inchture Tramway

1.5 miles approx., 4ft. 8½in. gauge. Owned by the Caledonian Railway Company. The passenger service was worked from 1895 until closure, believed to be late in 1916, by a solitary horse-drawn, single-deck saloon tramcar built at the Company's St. Rollox Works in Glasgow. Livery Crimson Lake and white.

Stirling and Bridge of Allan Tramways Co. Ltd.

4.35 miles, 4ft. 8½in. gauge, horse traction, opened 27 July 1874, closed 5 February 1920. Livery latterly red-brown and cream. A petrol car was also operated from 9 December 1913 until 20 May 1920.
Initially rolling stock was three cars, Nos. 1-2 open-top, knifeboard, and No. 3 single-deck, all supplied by the Tramway Carriage & Works Company of Glasgow in 1874. Nos. 4-6, single-deck toastracks followed in 1885. Nos. 5-6 were rebuilt locally and Nos. 4-5 probably renumbered 2-3(ii). No. 7 was obtained in 1887, probably ex-Edinburgh Street Tramways Co. It had an Eades reversible open-top body with knifeboard seating. Little is known about No. 4(ii) of 1888 and No. 8(ii) of 1894, both open-top with garden seats, possibly by Ashbury and Milnes respectively. At least seven open-top and three toastrack cars were obtained in later years; the former included No. 9 ex-Glasgow Tramway & Omnibus Co. Ltd. bought in 1895, Nos. 20-21 bought in 1900 and Nos. 22-23 bought in 1902, all ex-EDT. No. 22 was rebuilt as a petrol car in 1913. The three toastracks were No. 8 of 1894, No. 19 of 1900 and No. 24 of 1902, the two latter having locally-built bodies.

Leith Corporation's water car No. 60 was supplied by UEC in 1905. It was later Edinburgh Corporation grinder No. 1. *(Courtesy A. W. Brotchie)*

Leith Corporation Tramways

9.09 miles, 4ft. 8½in. gauge. Horse tramway acquired 23 October 1904, last horse tram 2 November 1905. Electric operation commenced 18 August 1905, to Edinburgh Corporation 2 November 1920. Livery Munich lake and cream.

Car numbers	Type (as built)	Year built	Builder	Seats	Truck(s)	Motors	Controllers
1-15 (a)(d)	Open top	1905	UEC	22/36	Brill 21E	GE 54-5T 2 x 25hp	BTH B18 5T
16-30 (b)(d)	Open top	1905	Brush	22/34	Brush AA	Brush 1002B 2 x 25hp	Brush 3A
31-33	Balcony	1905	UEC	22/34	Brill 21E	GE 54-5T 2 x 25hp	BTH B18
34-36 (d)	Balcony	1905	Brush	22/32	Brush AA	Brush 1002B 2 x 25hp	Brush 3A
37 (c)	Open top	1906	Brush	22/34	Brush AA ?	GE 54-5T 2 x 25hp	BTH B18
60	Water car	1905	UEC	—	Brill 21E	GE 58-6T 2 x 28hp	BTH B18

Notes

(a) Brush balcony top-covers fitted 1912-14. Nos. 2, 15 fitted new longer Brill 21E trucks in 1919.
(b) Brush balcony top-covers fitted to Nos. 16-19 in 1914.
(c) Delivered in 1905, (possibly from ER&TCW), as a single-deck instruction car, No. 61. Fitted with new Brush body in 1906, and Brush balcony top-cover in 1914.
(d) Nos. 8, 10, 15, 29, 35 fitted with platform vestibules 1913-15.

Kirkcaldy Corporation Tramways

6.11 miles, 3ft. 6in. gauge, opened 28 February 1903, closed 15 May 1931. Livery olive green and cream.

Car numbers	Type (as built)	Year built	Builder	Seats	Truck(s)	Motors	Controllers
1-10	Open top	1902	Milnes	22/26	Milnes Pressed steel	BTH GE58-6T 2 x 28hp	BTH B18
11-22	Open top	1903-04	Milnes	22/26	Milnes Pressed steel	BTH GE58-6T 2 x 28hp	BTH B18
23-26	Open top	1916	Hurst Nelson	22/26	Hurst Nelson Solid forged	BTH GE58-6T 2 x 28hp	BTH B18

Nos. 23-26 and four of Nos. 1-22 were sold on closure to Wemyss & District where the top decks were removed.

Musselburgh & District Electric Light and Traction Co. Ltd.

6.52 miles, 4ft. 8½in. gauge, opened 12 December 1904, regular services to Port Seton ceased 1 March 1928, workmens specials continued until 31 March 1928. Joppa-Levenhall section, 2.94 miles, operated by Edinburgh Corporation until purchased by them on 7 May 1931. Final closure 13 November 1954. Livery red and ivory, later dark and light green.

Car numbers	Type (as built	Year built	Builder	Seats	Truck(s)	Motors	Controllers
1-10	Open top	1904	UEC	22/32	BEC SB60	GE 54-3T 2 x 29hp	GE K10D
11-14 (a)	Open top	1905	Brush	22/35	M&G 21EM	GE 54-3T 2 x 29hp	GE K10D
15-16	Balcony	1909	Brush	22/36	M&G 21EM	GE 54-3T 2 x 29hp	GE K10D
17 (b)	Single-deck	Bought 1918	Brush	28	Brill 21E	GE 52-6T 2 x 20hp	BTH B13
18-19 (c)	Single-deck	Bought 1918	SCT	28	Brill 21E	GE 52-6T 2 x 20hp	BTH B13
20-22 (d)	Balcony	Bought 1923	Various	22/29	Brill 21E	GE 58-4T 2 x 37.5hp	BTH B13

Notes

(a) All top-covered by 1909. No.13 renumbered 5 c1917.
(b) Ex-Sheffield Corporation (SCT) No.94, built 1900.
(c) Ex-Sheffield Corporation Nos.203,210 respectively, built 1903.
(d) Ex-Sheffield Corporation Nos.141,170,25 built 1901-05 by Milnes, Cravens and SCT respectively.

Perth and District Tramways Co. Ltd.

4.26 miles, 3ft. 6in. gauge, opened 17 September 1895, purchased by Perth Corporation as from 7 October 1903. Last horse tram ran 31 October 1905. Livery dark crimson and cream. Total stock nine cars; 1-4 open top, garden seats, by Brown Marshalls; 5 single-deck cross-bench car by Brown Marshalls; 6-9 open top, garden seats, purchased later.

Perth Corporation Tramways

5.01 miles, 3ft. 6in. gauge, opened 31 October 1905, closed 19 January 1929. Livery crimson lake and cream; Nos. 10-12 originally dark olive green and cream.

Car numbers	Type (as built)	Year built	Builder	Seats	Truck(s)	Motors	Controllers
1-9	Open top	1905	Hurst Nelson	20/22	Hurst Nelson Solid forged	Westinghouse 2 x 25hp	Westinghouse
10-12	Open top Low bridge	1905	Hurst Nelson	20/22	Hurst Nelson Solid forged	Westinghouse 2 x 25hp	Westinghouse

Note: The motors were probably Type 46 and the controllers 90M.

The Wemyss and District Tramways Co. Ltd.

7.45 miles, 3ft. 6in. gauge, opened 25 August 1906, closed 30 January 1932. Livery mustard yellow, later maroon and yellow.

Car numbers	Type (as built)	Year built	Builder	Seats	Truck(s)	Motors	Controllers
1-13	Single-deck saloon	1906-7	Brush	28	Brush AA	Bruce Peebles 2 x 25hp	Bruce Peebles
14-17	Single-deck convertible	1907	Milnes Voss	50	M&G MxT bogies	BTH GE58-4T 2 x 37hp	BTH B18
18-19 (a)	Single-deck saloon	1925	Brush	45	Brush MxT bogies	BTH 249AA 2 x 37hp	BTH B18
20 (b)	Single-deck saloon	Bought 1928	Midland	40	M&G EqW bogies	GE 58-4T 2 x 37hp	GE K10
21 (b)	Single-deck saloon	Bought 1928	Brush	40	Brush EqW bogies	GE 58-4T 2 x 37hp	GE K10
22-29 (c)	Single-deck	Bought 1931	Hurst Nelson	22	(c)	BTH GE58-6T 2 x 28hp	BTH B18
1-2 (d)	Trailer/ Luggage van	Bought 1907	Brush	—	Trunions	—	—

Notes

(a) Sold to Dunfermline, their Nos. 45, 44 respectively.
(b) Bodies, built 1900, ex-Potteries Electric Traction Company.
(c) Ex-Kirkcaldy 23-26 and four from Nos. 1-10. Top deck seats and stairs were removed on arrival at Wemyss. Trucks were four Milnes pressed steel and four Hurst Nelson Solid forged.
(d) Ex-Potteries Electric Traction Company Ltd. Built 1902.

Four Kirkcaldy Corporation cars were hired in the early weeks of operation.

Key to Abbreviations and Manufacturers

ACT	—	Aberdeen Corporation Tramways, Dee Village or King Street works.
Arbel	—	Etablissements Arbel Forges, Douai, France.
Ashbury	—	The Ashbury Railway Carriage and Iron Co. Ltd., Manchester.
BEC	—	The British Electric Car Co. Ltd., Trafford Park, Manchester.
Brill	—	The J. G. Brill Company, Inc., Philadelphia, USA.
Brown Marshalls	—	Brown Marshall & Co. Ltd., Adderley Park, Birmingham.
Bruce Peebles	—	Bruce Peebles & Co. Ltd., East Pilton Works, Edinburgh.
Brush	—	The Brush Electrical Engineering Co. Ltd., Loughborough.
BTH	—	The British Thomson-Houston Company Ltd., Rugby.
CG de C	—	Compagnie Generale de Construction, St. Denis, Paris, France.
Cravens	—	Cravens Railway Carriage & Wagon Co. Ltd., Darnall, Sheffield.
DK	—	Dick, Kerr & Company Ltd., Preston.
DCT	—	Dundee Corporation Tramways, Lochee Road Works.
ECT	—	Edinburgh Corporation Tramways, Shrubhill Works.
E & DT	—	Edinburgh and District Tramways Company Ltd.
EE	—	English Electric Company Ltd., Preston, Lancashire.
EMB	—	The Electro-Mechanical Brake Co. Ltd., West Bromwich, Staffs.
EqW.	—	Equal-wheel bogies.
ER & TCW	—	The Electric Railway & Tramway Carriage Works Ltd., Preston.
Falcon	—	Falcon Engine & Car Works, Loughborough (predecessor of Brush).
Ganz	—	The Ganz Electric Company, Budapest, Hungary.
GE	—	The General Electric Company Inc., Schenectady, NY, USA.
GEC	—	General Electric Company Ltd., Witton Works, Birmingham.
GNSR	—	Great North of Scotland Railway, Kittybrewster Works, Aberdeen.
Green	—	Thomas Green & Son Ltd., Smithfield, Leeds.
HN	—	Hurst Nelson & Company Ltd., Motherwell, Scotland.
Kitson	—	Kitson & Company Ltd., Airedale Foundry, Leeds.
Leeds Forge	—	Leeds Forge Co. Ltd., Armley, Leeds (also at Bristol).
Lwt bogies	—	Lightweight bogies.
McHardy & Elliot	—	McHardy & Elliot Company Ltd., Edinburgh.
Metropolitan	—	The Metropolitan Railway Carriage & Wagon Co. Ltd., Saltley, Birmingham.
MC	—	Metropolitan-Cammell Co. Ltd., Saltley, Birmingham.
MCT	—	Manchester Corporation Tramways, Hyde Road Works.
Midland	—	Midland Railway Carriage & Wagon Co. Ltd., Shrewsbury, later Birmingham.
Milnes	—	G. F. Milnes & Co. Ltd., Birkenhead, later Hadley, Shropshire.
Milnes Voss	—	G. C. Milnes, Voss & Co. Ltd., Birkenhead.
M & T	—	Maley & Taunton Ltd., Wednesbury, Staffs.
M & G	—	Mountain & Gibson Ltd., Bury, Lancs.
MV	—	The Metropolitan-Vickers Electrical Co. Ltd., Trafford Park, Manchester.
MxT	—	Maximum Traction bogies.
PAYE	—	Pay as you Enter.
Peckham	—	Peckham Truck & Engineering Co. Ltd.
RYP	—	R. Y. Pickering & Co. Ltd., Wishaw, Lanarkshire.
SCT	—	Sheffield Corporation Tramways, Queens Road Works.
Siemens	—	Siemens Brothers Dynamo Works Ltd., Stafford.
Starbuck	—	Starbuck Car & Wagon Company Ltd., Birkenhead. (Later G. F. Milnes).
UEC	—	United Electric Car Company Ltd., Preston.
Westinghouse	—	Westinghouse Electric & Manufacturing Co. Inc., Pittsburg, USA.
Westinghouse	—	British Westinghouse Electric Co. Ltd., Trafford Park, Manchester.

The Electric Railway & Tramway Carriage Works Ltd. (renamed United Electric Car Co. Ltd. from 25 September 1905) was a subsidiary of Dick, Kerr & Co. Ltd., which merged with other electrical companies on 14 December 1918 to form the English Electric Company Ltd. Most post 1908 Peckham trucks were built by Brush, and also by HN, EE and EMB. Metropolitan-Vickers were successors to British Westinghouse.

Acknowledgements and Sources

This book is based on Chapter 13 of *Great British Tramway Networks* by W. H. Bett and J. C. Gillham (LRTL 1962) with additional information from recent books and articles, especially Edinburgh's Transport by the late D. L. G. Hunter and the various books on the Scottish systems published by NB Traction over several years. Duncan's Guide was consulted at Edinburgh Record Office for information on early horse and cable tramcar fleet details. The fleet lists have been compiled by R. J. S. Wiseman with the valuable assistance of A. W. Brotchie for Edinburgh and Dundee, Ian Souter for Aberdeen, and Philip Groves for advising and checking rolling stock equipment details. Rosie Thacker, Librarian at the National Tramway Museum, helped with source material and photographs.

The maps have been drawn by J. C. Gillham and R. A. Smith, the latter, except that of Cruden Bay, being based on information originally appearing in those drawn by A. W. Brotchie. Photographs have been reproduced by the kind permission of A. W. Brotchie, E. N. C. Haywood, Ian Souter and M. G. C. W. Wheeler. Also Aberdeen Transport Society, Dundee City Library, The National Tramway Museum, The Science Museum, London, and Roy Brook for the cover photographs.

Periodicals consulted have included *Modern Tramway, Tramway Review, Scottish Tramlines, The Light Railway and Tramway Journal, The Tramway and Railway World,* and *Modern Transport.*

Bibliography — General

Duncan's Manual, (T. J. Whiting & Sons Ltd.).
Great British Tramway Networks, by W. H. Bett and J. C. Gillham, (Light Railway Transport League, 4th Edition, 1962)
Scottish Tramway Fleets, by A. W. Brotchie, (NB Traction, 1968).
What Colour Was That Tram, by David Voice, (Author, 4th edition, 1998).

Aberdeen

Aberdeen Corporation Tramways, by M. J. Mitchell, (First Aberdeen, 1999).
Aberdeen District Tramways, by M. J. Mitchell and I. A. Souter (NB Traction, 1983).
Aberdeen Suburban Tramways, by M. J. Mitchell and I. A. Souter (NB Traction, 1980).
Aberdeen's Trams, 1874-1958, by H. R. MacKenzie and A. W. Brotchie (Scottish Tramway Museum Society/ N.B. Traction, 1974).

Cruden Bay Hotel Tramway

Cruden Bay Hotel Tramway, by M. J. Mitchell (in *Tramway Review* 122, Summer 1965).
Locomotives of the L.N.E.R. Part 10B, Railcars and Electric Stock, (RCTS 1990).

Dundee

Tramways of the Tay Valley, by A. W. Brotchie, (Dundee Museum, 1965).

Dunfermline

The Dunfermline and District Tramways Company, by A. W. Brotchie, (NB Traction, 1978).
Fife's Trams and Buses, by A. W. Brotchie, (NB Traction, 1990).

Edinburgh

Edinburgh's Transport by D. L. G. Hunter, (Advertiser Press, 1964).
Edinburgh's Transport, The Corporation Years, by D. L. G. Hunter, (Adam Gordon, 1999).
The Tramways of Leith, by William Allen, (in *Tramway Review* 86-88, 1976-77).

Opposite: The quality of the lighting and seating of modern tramcars is well illustrated by the upper saloon of Edinburgh Corporation No. 12, built in 1935 by Hurst Nelson.
(J. C. Gillham

Falkirk
The Tramways of Falkirk, by A. W. Brotchie, (NB Traction, 1975).
Fife's Trams and Buses, by A. W. Brotchie, (NB Traction, 1990).

Kirkcaldy
The Tramways of Kirkcaldy, by A. W. Brotchie, (NB Traction, 1978).
Fife's Trams and Buses, by A. W. Brotchie, (NB Traction, 1990).

Musselburgh
Edinburgh's Transport, by D. L. G. Hunter, (Advertiser Press, 1964).

Perth
Tramways of the Tay Valley, by A. W. Brotchie, (Dundee Museum, 1965).

Stirling
The Tramways of Stirling, by A. W. Brotchie, (NB Traction, 1976).
Stirling's Trams and Buses, by A. W. Brotchie, (NB Traction, 1991).

Wemyss
The Wemyss and District Tramways Co. Ltd., by Alan W. Brotchie, (NB Traction, 1976).
Fife's Trams and Buses, by A. W. Brotchie, (NB Traction, 1990).

Trams ran from Edinburgh Post Office to Levenhall for the last time on 13 November 1954. No. 148 is seen on the last day of operation. The cable track remains in situ as a memento to the trams. *(M. G. C. W. Wheeler*

Inside Back cover
Above A traditional tramway scene in Dundee High Street. Dundee 55, on the left, is loading for Downfield while 45 has come in from Ninewells. *(Roy Brook*
Below The Old Steeple (St. Mary's Tower of the City Churches) forms the backdrop as 29 stands in South Lindsay Street before turning into Nethergate to load passengers in 1955. *(Roy Brook*

Printed by W. J. Ray, Spectrum House, Leamore Lane, Walsall WS2 7DQ. Tel: (01922) 428267